SOCIAL ISSUES, JUSTICE AND STATUS

SOCIAL SECURITY: BACKGROUND, ISSUES AND PROPOSALS

Social Issues, Justice and Status

Additional books in this series can be found on Nova's website under the Series tab.

Additional E-books in this series can be found on Nova's website under the E-books tab.

Aging Issues, Health and Financial Alternatives

Additional books in this series can be found on Nova's website under the Series tab.

Additional E-books in this series can be found on Nova's website under the E-books tab.

SOCIAL ISSUES, JUSTICE AND STATUS

SOCIAL SECURITY: BACKGROUND, ISSUES AND PROPOSALS

JACOB T. ÁLVAREZ
EDITOR

Nova Science Publishers, Inc.
New York

For permission to use material from this book please contact us:
Telephone 631-231-7269; Fax 631-231-8175
Web Site: http://www.novapublishers.com

NOTICE TO THE READER

Additional color graphics may be available in the e-book version of this book.

LIBRARY OF CONGRESS CATALOGING-IN-PUBLICATION DATA
Social security : background, issues and proposals / editor, Jacob T. Alvarez.
p. cm.
Includes index.
ISBN 978-1-61761-469-9 (hbk.)
1. Social security--United States. I. Alvarez, Jacob T.
HD7125.S5966 2010
368.4'300973--dc22
2010043953

Published by Nova Science Publishers, Inc. † New York

CONTENTS

PREFACE

The Social Security program pays benefits to retired and disabled workers and their family members, and to family members of deceased workers. The Social Security program is financed primarily through payroll taxes that are deposited in the U.S. Treasury and credited to the Social Security trust fund. Any revenues credited to the trust fund in excess of program costs (benefit payments and administrative expenses) are invested in special U.S. government obligations (debt instruments of the U.S. government). This book examines the basics of how the Social Security program is funded and how the Social Security trust fund works.

Chapter 1- The Social Security program pays benefits to retired and disabled workers and their family members, and to family members of deceased workers. Program income and outgo are accounted for in two separate trust funds authorized under Title II of the Social Security Act: the Federal Old-Age and Survivors Insurance (OASI) trust fund and the Federal Disability Insurance (DI) trust fund. This chapter refers to the two trust funds as an aggregate Social Security trust fund and discusses the operations of the OASI and DI trust funds on a combined basis.

The Social Security program is financed primarily through payroll taxes that are deposited in the U.S. Treasury and credited to the Social Security trust fund. Any revenues credited to the trust fund in excess of program costs (benefit payments and administrative expenses) are invested in special U.S. government obligations (debt instruments of the U.S. government).

Chapter 2- The Social Security Act has always required surplus Social Security revenue (revenue in excess of the program's expenditures) to be invested in U.S. government securities (or U.S. government- backed securities). In recent years, however, attention has been focused on alternative investment practices in an effort to increase the interest earnings of the trust funds, among other goals. This chapter explains trust fund investment practices under current law.

Chapter 3- One issue that never seems far from the minds of policymakers is Social Security. At the heart of the issue is the large shortfall of projected revenues needed to meet the mounting costs of the system. For the moment, the amount of Social Security tax receipts exceeds the amount of benefits being paid out. The Social Security trustees estimate that, beginning in 2024, the amount of benefits being paid out will exceed tax collections. According to the trustees' best estimate, the trust fund will be exhausted in the year 2037.

Some have argued that because the Social Security trust fund is intended to meet rising future costs of the program, its surplus should not be counted as offsetting official measures of the budget deficit. With regard to current saving, however, it makes no difference whether the surplus is credited to the trust fund or simply seen as financing current federal government outlays (including Social Security benefits). Off-budget surpluses contribute to national saving in exactly the same way as on-budget surpluses do. The additional saving they represent adds to the national saving rate and allows current investment spending to be higher than it would otherwise be.

Chapter 4- Under the Social Security Retirement Earnings Test (RET), the monthly benefit of a Social Security beneficiary who is below full retirement age (FRA) is reduced if he or she has earnings that exceed an annual threshold. In 2010, a beneficiary who is below FRA and will not attain FRA during the year is subject to a $1 reduction in benefits for each $2 of earnings above $14,160. A beneficiary who will attain FRA in 2010 is subject to a $1 reduction in benefits for each $3 of earnings above $37,680. The annual exempt amounts ($14,160 and $37,680 in 2010) generally are adjusted each year according to average wage growth.

Chapter 5- Social Security taxes are levied on covered earnings up to a maximum level set each year. In 2010, this maximum—or what is referred to as the taxable earnings base—is $106,800. The taxable earnings base serves as both a cap on contributions and a cap on benefits. As a contribution base, it establishes the maximum amount of each worker's earnings that is subject to the payroll tax. As a benefit base, it establishes the maximum amount of earnings used to calculate benefits.

Since 1982, the Social Security taxable earnings base has risen at the same rate as average wages in the economy. However, because of increasing earnings inequality, the percentage of covered earnings that are taxable has decreased from 90% in 1982 to 85% in 2005. The percentage of covered earnings that is taxable is projected to decline to about 83% for 2014 and later. Because the cap was indexed to the average growth in wages, the share of the population below the cap has remained relatively stable at roughly 94%. Of the 9.5 million Americans with earnings above the base, roughly 80% are men and only 9% had any earnings from self-employment income. The District of Columbia has the highest share of the population above the maximum (12%) and South Dakota has the lowest share (2%).

Chapter 6- According to the Social Security Trustees, assets in the two Social Security trust funds will be exhausted by 2037, and, thereafter, Social Security payroll tax revenues will cover about three-quarters of promised benefits. Over the past decade several proposals have been put forward which could help to close the Social Security program's long-term financing gap. One proposal would increase the Social Security payroll tax base so that 90% of covered earnings are taxable— the same proportion as in 1982. This policy would increase the payroll taxes paid by higher- earning workers and not affect workers earning less than the current Social Security maximum taxable limit, which is $106,800 in 2010.

Some analysts have proposed raising the Social Security payroll tax base and reducing the payroll tax rate. This policy would increase the taxes paid by higher-earning workers and reduce taxes paid by low- and middle-income workers. This policy proposal could raise revenue for the Social Security program or be revenue neutral.

Chapter 7- Social Security provides monthly benefits to qualified retirees, disabled workers, and their spouses and dependents. Until 1984, Social Security benefits were exempt from the federal income tax. In 1983, Congress approved recommendations from the National Commission on Social Security Reform (also known as the Greenspan Commission) to tax Social Security benefits above a specified income threshold. Specifically, beginning in 1984, up to 50% of Social Security and Railroad Retirement Board (RRB) Tier 1 benefits are taxable for individuals whose provisional income exceeds $25,000. The threshold is $32,000 for married couples. Provisional income is defined as the total income from all sources recognized for tax purposes plus certain otherwise tax-exempt income, including half of Social Security and RRB Tier 1 benefits. The proceeds from taxing Social Security and Railroad Retirement Tier I benefits at the 50% rate are credited to the Old-Age and Survivors Insurance (OASI) trust fund, the Disability Insurance (DI) trust fund, and the Railroad Retirement system respectively, based on the source of the benefit taxed.

Chapter 8- Most Social Security beneficiaries pay Medicare premiums. Beneficiaries who participate in Medicare Part B (Supplementary Medical Insurance) or Part D (prescription drugs) must pay monthly premiums, unless they qualify for low-income assistance. Part B participants who also receive Social Security must have the Part B premiums automatically deducted from their Social Security checks. Part D participants may choose to have their premiums deducted from their Social Security checks.

Medicare premiums are absorbing a growing share of Social Security benefits. To see the effect of growing premiums, consider a Social Security beneficiary who earned the average wage throughout his or her career. If this retiree chose to participate in Part B—as the vast majority of Social Security beneficiaries do—the standard Part B premium would have absorbed almost 5% of benefits upon retirement in 2000 and about 8.5% in 2010 after over a decade of retirement. For a new retiree in 2010, the Part B premium absorbs about 9% of the Social Security benefit, and combined premiums for both Part B and Part D absorb about 12% of the average initial Social Security benefit check. Medicare's trustees project that premiums for Parts B and D will grow at a faster rate than average Social Security benefits in the future, thus consuming a greater proportion of benefits over time. In 2078, a retired worker receiving the average initial Social Security benefit amount is projected to need 22% of benefits to pay the Part B premium and 31% of initial benefits to pay combined Parts B and D premiums.

In: Social Security: Background, Issues and... ISBN: 978-1-61761-469-9
Editors: Jacob T. Álvarez

Chapter 1

SOCIAL SECURITY: THE TRUST FUND

Dawn Nuschler and Gary Sidor

SUMMARY

The Social Security program pays benefits to retired and disabled workers and their family members, and to family members of deceased workers. Program income and outgo are accounted for in two separate trust funds authorized under Title II of the Social Security Act: the Federal Old-Age and Survivors Insurance (OASI) trust fund and the Federal Disability Insurance (DI) trust fund. This chapter refers to the two trust funds as an aggregate Social Security trust fund and discusses the operations of the OASI and DI trust funds on a combined basis.

The Social Security program is financed primarily through payroll taxes that are deposited in the U.S. Treasury and credited to the Social Security trust fund. Any revenues credited to the trust fund in excess of program costs (benefit payments and administrative expenses) are invested in special U.S. government obligations (debt instruments of the U.S. government).

The Social Security trust fund represents funds dedicated to pay current and future Social Security benefits. However, it is useful to view the trust fund in two ways: (1) as an internal federal accounting concept, and (2) as the accumulated holdings of the Social Security program.

For internal accounting purposes, certain accounts within the U.S. Treasury are designated by law as trust funds to track revenues (and expenditures) dedicated for specific purposes. There are a number of trust funds in the U.S. Treasury, including those for Social Security, Medicare, unemployment compensation, and federal employee retirement.

By law, any surplus Social Security revenues must be invested in U.S. government obligations. The accumulated holdings of U.S. government obligations are often viewed as being similar to assets held by any other trust on behalf of the beneficiaries. However, the holdings of the Social Security trust fund differ from those of private trusts because (1) the types of investments the trust fund may hold are limited, and (2) the U.S. government is both the buyer and seller of the investments.

This chapter covers the basics of how the Social Security program is funded and how the Social Security trust fund works.

INTRODUCTION

The Social Security program pays benefits to retired and disabled workers and their family members, and to family members of deceased workers. The program is financed primarily through payroll taxes that are deposited in the U.S. Treasury and credited to the Social Security trust fund. Any revenues credited to the trust fund in excess of program costs (benefit payments and administrative expenses) are invested in special U.S. government obligations (debt instruments of the U.S. government). The Social Security trust fund is both a designated account within the U.S. Treasury and the accumulated holdings of special U.S. government obligations. Both represent the funds designated to pay current and future Social Security benefits.

HOW THE SOCIAL SECURITY PROGRAM IS FINANCED

The Social Security program is financed primarily by revenues from Federal Insurance Contributions Act (FICA) taxes and Self Employment Contributions Act (SECA) taxes. FICA taxes are paid by both employers and employees, but it is employers who remit the taxes to the U.S. Treasury. Employers remit FICA taxes on a regular basis throughout the year (for example, weekly, monthly, quarterly or annually), depending on the employer's level of total employment taxes (including FICA and federal personal income tax withholding). The FICA tax rate of 7.65% each for employers and employees has two components: 6.2% for Social Security and 1.45% for Medicare Hospital Insurance. In 2009, employers and employees each pay 6.2% of wages up to $106,800 in Social Security payroll taxes.[1] The SECA tax rate is 15.3% for self-employed individuals, with 12.4% for Social Security and 2.9% for Medicare Hospital Insurance. In 2009, self-employed individuals pay 12.4% of net self-employment income up to $106,800 in Social Security payroll taxes, with one-half of the SECA taxes allowed as a deduction for federal income tax purposes.[2] SECA taxes are normally paid once a year as part of filing an annual individual income tax return.

In addition to Social Security payroll taxes, the Social Security program has two other sources of income. Certain Social Security recipients must include a portion of Social Security benefits in taxable income for the federal income tax, and the Social Security program receives part of those taxes.[3] In addition, the Social Security program receives interest from the U.S. Treasury on its investments in special U.S. government obligations.

The Internal Revenue Service (IRS) processes the tax returns and tax payments for federal employment taxes and federal individual income taxes. All of the tax payments are deposited in the U.S. Treasury along with all other receipts from the public for the federal government.

THE SOCIAL SECURITY TRUST FUND AS A DESIGNATED ACCOUNT

Within the U.S. Treasury, there are numerous accounts established for internal accounting purposes. Although all of the monies within the Treasury are federal monies, the designation of an account as a trust fund allows the government to track revenues (and expenditures) dedicated for specific purposes. In addition, the government can affect the level of revenues and expenditures associated with a trust fund through changes in the law. Social Security program income and outgo are accounted for in two separate trust funds authorized under Title II of the Social Security Act: the Federal Old-Age and Survivors Insurance (OASI) trust fund and (2) the Federal Disability Insurance (DI) trust fund.[4] This chapter refers to the two separate trust funds as an aggregate Social Security trust fund and discusses the operations of the OASI and DI trust funds on a combined basis.

Social Security Trust Fund Revenues

The Social Security trust fund receives a credit equal to the Social Security payroll taxes deposited in the U.S. Treasury by the IRS. The payroll taxes are allocated between the OASI and DI trust funds based on a proportion specified by law.[5] Currently, of the 6.2% tax rate, 5.3% is allocated to the OASI trust fund and 0.9% is allocated to the DI trust fund.[6]

Social Security Trust Fund Costs

The U. S. Treasury makes Social Security benefit payments to entitled individuals on a monthly basis. The Treasury is directed by the Social Security Administration (SSA) as to whom to pay and the amount of the payment. When benefit payments are made by the Treasury, the Social Security trust fund is debited for the payments. Periodically, the Social Security trust fund is also debited for the administrative costs of the Social Security program. These administrative costs are incurred by several government agencies, including SSA, the U.S. Treasury, and the IRS.

Social Security Trust Fund Operations

The annual revenues to the Social Security trust fund are used to pay current Social Security benefits and administrative expenses. If, in any year, revenues are greater than costs, the Secretary of the Treasury (as the Managing Trustee of the Social Security trust fund) is *required* to invest surplus Social Security revenues in securities backed by the U.S. government.[7] The purchase of government securities allows surplus Social Security revenues to be used for other government spending needs at the time.[8] If, in any year, costs are greater than revenues, the cash flow deficit is offset by selling some of the accumulated holdings of the trust fund (government securities) to pay benefits and administrative expenses.

There are two measures of Social Security trust fund operations: the annual cash flow operations and the accumulated holdings (or trust fund balance).[9] The annual cash flow operations of the Social Security trust fund are a measure of current revenues and current costs. The cash flow operations are positive when current revenues exceed costs (a cash flow surplus) and negative when current costs exceed revenues (a cash flow deficit). In years with cash flow deficits, the Social Security program (unlike other federal programs that operate without a trust fund) may use the accumulated holdings of the Social Security trust fund from prior years to pay benefits and administrative expenses.[10]

Although Social Security is often referred to as a pay-as-you-go system (meaning that current revenues are used to pay current costs), changes made to the Social Security program in 1983, including the coverage of federal workers, an increase in the full retirement age, and the taxation of Social Security benefits, began a sustained period of annual cash flow surpluses. In the 2009 Annual Report, the Social Security trustees project annual cash flow surpluses to continue through 2015. Beginning in 2016, however, program costs are projected to exceed revenues and annual cash flow deficits are projected to continue throughout the remainder of the 75-year projection period (under the intermediate assumptions).[11]

On average, over the 75-year projection period (2009 to 2083), the Social Security trustees project that program costs will exceed income (tax revenues plus interest income) by an amount equal to 2.00% of taxable payroll (costs are projected to exceed income by 14%).[12] The gap between income and costs, however, is projected to increase over the 75-year projection period. For example, in 2030, the cost of the program is projected to exceed income by an amount equal to 3.56% of taxable payroll (costs are projected to exceed income by 27%). By the end of the projection period, in 2083, the cost of the program is projected to exceed income by an amount equal to 4.34% of taxable payroll (costs are projected to exceed income by 33%). According to the Social Security trustees, the Social Security program could be brought into actuarial balance over the next 75 years with changes equivalent to an immediate 16% increase in the payroll tax (from a rate of 12.4% to 14.4%) or an immediate reduction in benefits of 13% (or some combination of the two options). The Social Security trustees point out that larger changes would be needed to maintain trust fund solvency beyond the next 75 years.[13]

As shown in Table 1, during the 1957 to 1983 period, the cash flow operations of the Social Security trust fund (annual revenues less annual costs) were negative in 21 of the 27 years.

Table 1. Annual Revenues, Costs, and Cash Flow Surplus or Deficit for the Social Security Trust Fund, 1957-1983 ($ in billions)

Year	Annual Revenues (not including interest)	Annual Costs	Annual Cash Flow Surplus or Deficit (annual revenues less annual costs)
1957	$7.50	$7.60	($0.10)
1958	8.50	8.90	(0.40)
1959	8.90	10.80	(1.90)
1960	11.90	11.80	0.10
1961	12.30	13.40	(1.10)
1962	13.10	15.20	(2.10)
1963	15.60	16.20	(0.60)
1964	16.80	17.00	(0.20)
1965	17.20	19.20	(2.00)
1966	22.60	20.90	1.70
1967	25.40	22.50	2.90
1968	27.00	26.00	1.00
1969	31.50	27.90	3.60
1970	34.70	33.10	1.60
1971	38.30	38.50	(0.20)
1972	42.90	43.30	(0.40)
1973	51.90	53.10	(1.20)
1974	58.90	60.60	(1.70)
1975	64.30	69.20	(4.90)
1976	71.60	78.20	(6.60)
1977	78.70	87.30	(8.60)
1978	88.90	96.00	(7.10)
1979	103.00	107.30	(4.30)
1980	116.70	123.60	(6.90)
1981	139.40	144.40	(5.00)
1982	145.70	160.10	(14.40)
1983	156.30	171.20	(14.90)

Source: Table prepared by the Congressional Research Service (CRS) from data provided in *The 2009 Annual Report of the Board of Trustees of the Federal Old-Age and Survivors Insurance and Federal Disability Insurance Trust Funds*, Washington, DC, May 12, 2009, Table VI.A4.

Table 2. Annual Revenues, Costs, and Cash Flow Surplus for the Social Security Trust Fund, 1984-2008 ($ in billions)

Year	Annual Revenues (not including interest)	Annual Costs	Annual Cash Flow Surplus (annual revenues less annual costs)
1984	$183.10	$180.40	$2.70
1985	197.50	190.60	6.90
1986	212.80	201.50	11.30
1987	225.60	209.10	16.50
1988	255.20	222.50	32.70
1989	276.70	236.20	40.50
1990	301.10	253.10	48.00
1991	307.80	274.20	33.60
1992	317.20	291.90	25.30
1993	327.70	308.80	18.90
1994	350.00	323.00	27.00
1995	364.80	339.80	25.00
1996	385.70	353.60	32.10
1997	413.90	369.10	44.80
1998	439.90	382.30	57.60
1999	471.20	392.90	78.30
2000	504.80	415.10	89.70
2001	529.10	438.90	90.20
2002	546.30	461.70	84.60
2003	546.90	479.10	67.80
2004	568.70	501.60	67.10
2005	607.80	529.90	77.90
2006	642.50	555.40	87.10
2007	674.70	594.50	80.20
2008	689.00	625.10	63.90

Source: Table prepared by the Congressional Research Service (CRS) from data provided in *The 2009 Annual Report of the Board of Trustees of the Federal Old-Age and Survivors Insurance and Federal Disability Insurance Trust Funds*, Washington, DC, May 12, 2009, Table VI.A4.

Table 2 shows the cash flow operations of the Social Security trust fund (annual revenues, costs, and cash flow surplus) for the 1984 to 2008 period.

Table 3 shows the projected cash flow operations of the Social Security trust fund (projected annual revenues, costs, and cash flow surplus or deficit) for the 2009 to 2036 period, as projected by the Social Security trustees in the 2009 Annual Report (under the intermediate assumptions).

One way to measure the annual cash flow operations over time is to take the ratio of current revenues to current costs for each year. A ratio greater than 100% indicates positive cash flow (a cash flow surplus). Conversely, a ratio less than 100% indicates negative cash flow (a cash flow deficit). Figure 1 shows the ratio of current revenues to current costs for the Social Security trust fund over the historical period from 1957 to 2008 and over the future period from 2009 to 2036, as projected by the Social Security trustees in the 2009 Annual Report (under the intermediate assumptions).[14]

Table 3. Projected Annual Revenues, Costs, and Cash Flow Surplus or Deficit for the Social Security Trust Fund, 2009-2036 ($ in billions)

Year[a]	Annual Revenues (not including interest)	Annual Costs	Annual Cash Flow Surplus or Deficit (annual revenues less annual costs)
2009	$701.30	$682.50	$18.80
2010	727.60	709.30	18.30
2011	763.60	735.10	28.50
2012	810.40	772.40	38.00
2013	855.50	822.70	32.80
2014	898.60	880.20	18.40
2015	943.50	941.20	2.30
2016	986.40	1,005.30	(18.90)
2017	1,031.40	1,074.30	(42.90)
2018	1,077.00	1,147.50	(70.50)
2019	1,125.20	1,226.20	(101.00)
2020	1,175.50	1,308.80	(133.30)
2021	1,227.90	1,394.30	(166.40)
2022	1,282.50	1,482.40	(199.90)
2023	1,339.60	1,574.10	(234.50)
2024	1,399.10	1,669.40	(270.30)
2025	1,461.30	1,767.90	(306.60)
2026	1,526.00	1,869.50	(343.50)
2027	1,593.70	1,974.90	(381.20)
2028	1,664.40	2,083.70	(419.30)
2029	1,738.50	2,194.60	(456.10)

Table 3. (Continued)

Year[a]	Annual Revenues (not including interest)	Annual Costs	Annual Cash Flow Surplus or Deficit (annual revenues less annual costs)
2030	1,815.90	2,309.30	(493.40)
2031	1,897.00	2,426.80	(529.80)
2032	1,981.80	2,547.20	(565.40)
2033	2,070.30	2,670.00	(599.70)
2034	2,162.80	2,795.10	(632.30)
2035	2,259.20	2,922.90	(663.70)
2036	2,360.00	3,054.40	(694.40)

Source: Table prepared by the Congressional Research Service (CRS) from data provided in *The 2009 Annual Report of the Board of Trustees of the Federal Old-Age and Survivors Insurance and Federal Disability Insurance Trust Funds*, Washington, DC, May 12, 2009, Table VI.F8 (intermediate assumptions).

a. Projections for years after 2036 are not shown because the Social Security trust fund is projected to be exhausted in 2037 under the intermediate assumptions.

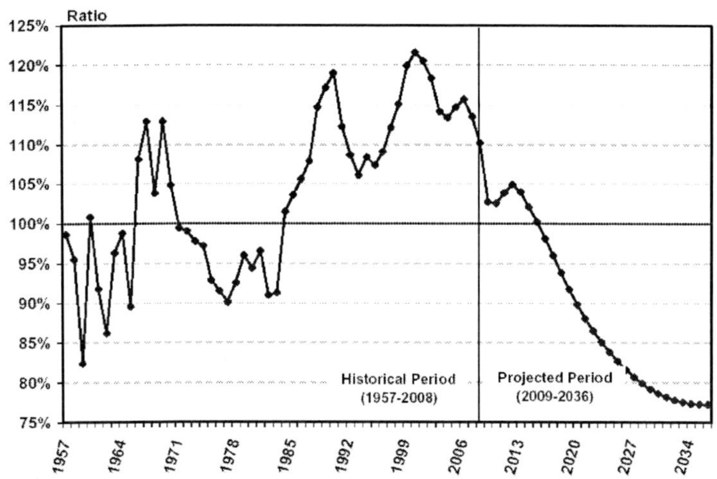

Source: Figure prepared by the Congressional Research Service (CRS) from data provided in *The 2009 Annual Report of the Board of Trustees of the Federal Old-Age and Survivors Insurance and Federal Disability Insurance Trust Funds*, Washington, DC, May 12, 2009, Tables VI.A4 and VI.F8 (intermediate assumptions).

Notes: Annual revenues do not include interest on accumulated holdings of U.S. government obligations. A ratio above 100% indicates a cash flow surplus for the year. A ratio below 100% indicates a cash flow deficit.

Figure 1. Ratio of Current (Annual) Revenues to Costs for the Social Security Trust Fund, 1957-2036

As shown in the figure, in 2008, revenues of $689 billion divided by costs of $625 billion results in a ratio of 110%, indicating a cash flow surplus for the Social Security trust fund. By comparison, in 2016, projected revenues of $986 billion divided by projected costs of $1 trillion results in a ratio of 98%, indicating a cash flow deficit. In the 2009 Annual Report, the Social Security trustees project that the ratio of current revenues to current costs will fall below 100% in 2016 and remain below 100% for the rest of the projection period, with the gap between revenues and costs increasing over time (under the intermediate assumptions).

While the Social Security program has experienced cash flow deficits in the past and is projected to do so in the future, Social Security benefits can continue to be paid by the Treasury at levels scheduled under current law as long as the accumulated balance in the Social Security trust fund is positive. This is because the Social Security program has budget authority to pay benefits as long as the balance in the Social Security trust fund (the designated account) is positive. However, when current revenues are not sufficient to pay benefits, the U.S. government must raise the funds necessary to honor the redemption of U.S. government obligations held by the Social Security trust fund as they are needed to pay benefits. If there are no surplus governmental receipts, the U.S. government may raise the necessary funds by increasing taxes or other income, reducing spending, or borrowing (or some combination of these options).

Investment of the Social Security Trust Fund

The Secretary of the Treasury is required by law to invest Social Security revenues that are not needed to pay current benefits and administrative expenses in securities backed by the U.S. government.[15] In addition, the Social Security trust fund receives interest on its holdings of special U.S. government obligations. Each government security issued by the Treasury for purchase by the Social Security trust fund must be a paper instrument in the form of a bond, note or certificate of indebtedness.[16] Any interest or proceeds from the sale of government securities held by the Social Security trust fund must be paid in the form of paper checks from the general fund of the Treasury to the Social Security trust fund.[17] The interest rates paid on the government securities issued to the Social Security trust fund are tied to market rates.[18]

For internal federal accounting purposes, when special U.S. government obligations are purchased by the Social Security trust fund, the Treasury is shifting surplus Social Security revenues from one government account (the Social Security trust fund) to another government account (the Treasury's "general fund" account). The special U.S. government obligations are physical documents held by the Social Security Administration, not the U.S. Treasury. The government securities held by the Social Security trust fund are redeemed on a regular basis. These special U.S. government obligations, however, are not resources for the government because they represent both an asset and a liability for the government.

The Social Security Trust Fund and the Federal Budget

The Social Security program is indirectly part of the annual congressional budget process. This creates some confusion on the part of the public.

On-Budget versus Off-Budget

For federal budget purposes, *on-budget* status generally refers to programs that are included in the annual congressional budget process, whereas *off-budget* status generally refers to programs that are not included in the annual congressional budget process.

The Social Security program is a government program that, like the Postal Service, has had its receipts and (most) outlays designated by law as off-budget.[19] The off-budget designation, however, has no practical effect on program funding, spending, or operations. The annual congressional budget resolution, in its legislative language, separates the off-budget totals (receipts and outlays) from the on-budget totals (receipts and outlays). The report language accompanying the congressional budget resolution usually shows the unified budget totals (which combine the on- and off-budget amounts) as well as the separate on- and off-budget totals. The President's budget tends to use the unified budget measures in discussing the budget totals. The President's budget documents also include the totals for the on- and off-budget components, as required by law. The Congressional Budget Office uses the unified budget numbers in its analyses of the budget; it generally does not include on- and off-budget data in its regular annual reports.

The unified budget framework is important because it includes all federal government revenues and expenditures providing a more comprehensive picture of the size of the federal government, as well as the impact of the federal budget on the economy. In the unified budget, the Social Security program is a large source of both federal government revenues (26.1% in FY2008) and expenditures (20.7% in FY2008).[20] For purposes of the unified budget, the annual Social Security cash flow surplus or deficit is counted in determining the overall federal budget surplus or deficit.

THE SOCIAL SECURITY TRUST FUND AS ACCUMULATED HOLDINGS

The Social Security trust fund can be (and often is) viewed as a trust fund, similar to any private trust fund, that is to be used for paying current and future benefits (and administrative expenses). By law, any Social Security revenues credited to the trust fund (within the U.S. Treasury) in excess of program costs are invested in non-marketable U.S. government obligations. These obligations are physical (paper) documents issued to the trust fund and held by the Social Security Administration. When the obligations are redeemed, the Treasury must issue a check (a physical document) to the Social Security trust fund for the interest earned on the obligations.[21]

However, unlike a private trust that may hold a variety of assets and obligations of different borrowers, the Social Security trust fund can hold only non-marketable U.S. government obligations. The sale of these obligations by the U.S. government to the Social Security trust fund is federal government borrowing (from itself) and counts against the federal debt limit. The requirement that the Social Security trust fund purchase U.S. government obligations serves several purposes, such as:

- offering a mechanism for the Social Security program to recoup the surplus revenues loaned to the rest of the government,
- paying interest so that the loan of the surplus revenues does not lose value over time,
- ensuring that the Social Security trust fund (and not other government accounts) receives credit for the interest earnings,
- ensuring a level of return (interest) to the Social Security trust fund, and
- providing a means outside of the securities market for the U.S. government to borrow funds.

Table 4. Accumulated Holdings of the Social Security Trust Fund, 1957-2008 ($ in billions)

Year	Accumulated Holdings[a]
1957	$23.00
1958	23.20
1959	22.00
1960	22.60
1961	22.20
1962	20.70
1963	20.70
1964	21.20
1965	19.80
1966	22.30
1967	26.30
1968	28.70
1969	34.20
1970	38.10
1971	40.40
1972	42.80
1973	44.40
1974	45.90
1975	44.30
1976	41.10
1977	35.90
1978	31.70
1979	30.30
1980	26.50
1981	24.50
1982	24.80
1983	24.90
1984	31.10
1985	42.20
1986	46.90
1987	68.80
1988	109.80
1989	163.00

Table 4. (Continued)

Year	Accumulated Holdings[a]
1990	225.30
1991	280.70
1992	331.50
1993	378.30
1994	436.40
1995	496.10
1996	567.00
1997	655.50
1998	762.50
1999	896.10
2000	1,049.40
2001	1,212.50
2002	1,378.00
2003	1,530.80
2004	1,686.80
2005	1,858.70
2006	2,048.10
2007	2,238.50
2008	2,418.70

Source: Table prepared by the Congressional Research Service (CRS) from data provided in *The 2009 Annual Report of the Board of Trustees of the Federal Old-Age and Survivors Insurance and Federal Disability Insurance Trust Funds*, Washington, DC, May 12, 2009, Table VI.A4.

a. The accumulated holdings of the Social Security trust fund are also referred to as the trust fund balance.

The accumulated holdings of the Social Security trust fund represent the sum of annual surplus Social Security revenues (for all past years) which were invested in U.S. government obligations, plus the interest earned on those obligations. As a result of surplus Social Security revenues for the past 25 years (1984 to 2008) and the interest income credited to the Social Security trust fund, the accumulated holdings of the Social Security trust fund totaled $2.4 trillion at the end of calendar year 2008. It is the accumulated holdings of the Social Security trust fund (or the trust fund balance) that many people refer to when discussing the Social Security trust fund. **Table 4** shows the accumulated holdings of the Social Security trust fund for the historical period from 1957 to 2008. Table 5 shows the accumulated holdings of the Social Security trust fund for the future period from 2009 to 2036, as projected by the Social Security trustees in the 2009 Annual Report (under the intermediate assumptions). The Social Security trustees project that the level of accumulated holdings will begin to decline in 2024 and that the Social Security trust fund will be exhausted in 2037.

Table 5. Projected Accumulated Holdings of the Social Security Trust Fund, 2009-2036 ($ in billions)

Year[a]	Accumulated Holdings[b]
2009	$2,555.50
2010	2,693.90
2011	2,848.80
2012	3,022.90
2013	3,204.00
2014	3,383.50
2015	3,558.10
2016	3,722.40
2017	3,873.80
2018	4,008.80
2019	4,123.60
2020	4,215.40
2021	4,282.30
2022	4,322.20
2023	4,332.40
2024	4,306.60
2025	4,242.00
2026	4,135.90
2027	3,985.00
2028	3,786.10
2029	3,538.00
2030	3,237.20
2031	2,881.70
2032	2,469.30
2033	1,997.90
2034	1,465.70
2035	870.50
2036	209.50

Source: Table prepared by the Congressional Research Service (CRS) from data provided in *The 2009 Annual Report of the Board of Trustees of the Federal Old-Age and Survivors Insurance and Federal Disability Insurance Trust Funds*, Washington, DC, May 12, 2009, Table VI.F8 (intermediate assumptions).

a. Projections for years after 2036 are not shown because the Social Security trust fund is projected to be exhausted in 2037 under the intermediate assumptions.

b. The accumulated holdings of the Social Security trust fund are also referred to as the trust fund balance.

The Social Security Trust Fund and the Level of Federal Debt

As part of the annual congressional budget process, the level of federal debt (the federal debt limit) is set for the budget by Congress. The federal debt limit includes debt held by the public as well as the internal debt of the U.S. government (i.e., debt held by government accounts). Borrowing from the public and the investment of the Social Security trust fund in special U.S. government obligations both fall under the restrictions of the federal debt limit. This means that the Social Security trust fund balance may have implications for the federal debt limit. The sale of government securities to the Social Security trust fund is a transaction between federal accounts; it does not generate any resources for the government. It is the interest payments on federal debt held by the public that is considered the more relevant measure of the impact of the federal budget on the economy.

The Social Security Trust Fund and Federal Default

The special obligations purchased by the Social Security trust fund are backed by "the full faith and credit" of the U.S. government. This is a promise by the U.S. government to redeem the securities (debt instruments). Technically, like any other borrower, the federal government could default on any or all of its outstanding obligations. The implications for the economy, and for the private market for government securities, of a federal government default on the special obligations held by the Social Security trust fund would depend on the views of private investors. The impact would be determined by whether private investors think this is a precursor to a federal government default on securities held by the public (a general government default). There is no precedent for a federal government default which makes it difficult to predict the implications.

The Social Security Trust Fund and Benefit Payments

The accumulated holdings of the Social Security trust fund, which represent budget authority for the program, can be viewed as a measure of funds dedicated to pay current and future benefits. However, beginning in 2016, when revenues are projected to be below levels needed to pay benefits,[22] these funds will be available to pay benefits only as the government raises the resources necessary to pay for the securities as they are redeemed by the Social Security trust fund. The securities are a promise, by the U.S. government, to raise the necessary funds.[23] When the system is operating with a cash flow surplus, the surplus Social Security revenues (which are invested in government securities held by the trust fund) are used to fund other government activities at the time. The surplus Social Security revenues, therefore, are not available to finance benefits directly when the system is operating with a cash flow deficit.

The Social Security trustees project that the accumulated holdings of the Social Security trust fund will be exhausted in 2037 and that only an estimated 76% of scheduled annual benefits will be payable with incoming receipts at that point (based on the intermediate assumptions of the 2009 Annual Report). The Social Security Act does not state what would happen to the payment of benefits in the event of Social Security trust fund exhaustion. Two possible scenarios are the payment of full monthly benefits on a delayed schedule or the payment of partial (reduced) monthly benefits on time.[24]

End Notes

[1] The limit on wages subject to the Social Security payroll tax is indexed annually to average wage growth. The Medicare Hospital Insurance component of the FICA tax is levied on total wages.

[2] Self-employed individuals are required to pay Social Security payroll taxes if they have annual net earnings of $400 or more. Only 92.35% of net self-employment income (up to the annual limit) is taxable.

[3] The taxes associated with including Social Security benefits in federal taxable income go to the Social Security trust fund and the Medicare Hospital Insurance trust fund. See CRS Report RL32552, *Social Security: Calculation and History of Taxing Benefits*, by Janemarie Mulvey and Christine Scott.

[4] Social Security Act, Title II, §201.

[5] Social Security Act, Title II, §201(b).

[6] The share allocated to the DI trust fund was last changed (to 0.9%) in 2000. The proportional split between the OASI and DI trust funds has been altered five times since 1985.

[7] Social Security Act, Title II, §201(d).

[8] This is often referred to as "borrowing from the Social Security trust fund."

[9] The accumulated holdings of the Social Security trust fund in U.S. government obligations are often referred to as the Social Security trust fund balance.

[10] Certain government projects may be given "budget authority until expended," which allows the authority to spend funds on the project to be carried over each year until all of the authority to spend funds has been exhausted.

[11] *The 2009 Annual Report of the Board of Trustees of the Federal Old-Age and Survivors Insurance and Federal Disability Insurance Trust Funds*, Washington, DC, May 12, 2009.

[12] Program costs and income are evaluated as a percentage of taxable payroll because Social Security payroll taxes are the primary source of funding for the program. The projected 75-year actuarial deficit (2.00% of taxable payroll) represents $5.3 trillion in present value terms.

[13] Projections by the Social Security trustees are based on the intermediate assumptions of the 2009 Annual Report.

[14] *The 2009 Annual Report of the Board of Trustees of the Federal Old-Age and Survivors Insurance and Federal Disability Insurance Trust Funds*, Washington, DC, May 12, 2009, Tables VI.A4 & VI.F8 (intermediate assumptions).

[15] Social Security Act, Title II, §201(d).

[16] Social Security Act, Title II, §201(d). The Social Security trust fund may purchase certain other government securities, such as those issued by Fannie Mae or Freddie Mac, but this option is seldom used.

[17] Social Security Act, Title II, §201(f). The funds are then used to purchase additional government securities credited to the Social Security trust fund.

[18] For more information, see CRS Report RS20607, *Social Security: Trust Fund Investment Practices*, by Dawn Nuschler.

[19] Although the Social Security program is off-budget, the annual congressional budget process does provide the budget authority for Social Security administrative spending. SSA's administrative funding, which is paid for out of the Social Security trust fund, is subject to an annual appropriated limit. In contrast, the Social Security program has budget authority to pay benefits as long as the balance in the Social Security trust fund (the designated account) is positive.

[20] Percentages calculated by the Congressional Research Service (CRS) from data provided in: Office of Management and Budget, *Historical Tables, Budget of the U.S. Government, Fiscal Year 2010*, Tables 2.1, 2.4, 6.1 and 13.1.

[21] The funds are then used to purchase additional government securities credited to the Social Security trust fund.

[22] The Social Security trustees project that revenues will fall below program costs beginning in 2016, based on the intermediate assumptions of the 2009 Annual Report.

[23] If there are no surplus governmental receipts, policymakers would have three options: raise taxes or other income, reduce spending, or borrow (or some combination of these options).

[24] For information on the legal entitlement to benefits and trust fund exhaustion, see CRS Report RL32822, *Social Security Reform: Legal Analysis of Social Security Benefit Entitlement Issues*, by Kathleen S. Swendiman and Thomas J. Nicola, and CRS Report RL33514, *Social Security: What Would Happen If the Trust Funds Ran Out?*, by Kathleen Romig.

In: Social Security: Background, Issues and... ISBN: 978-1-61761-469-9
Editors: Jacob T. Álvarez

Chapter 2

SOCIAL SECURITY: TRUST FUND INVESTMENT PRACTICES

Dawn Nuschler

SUMMARY

The Social Security Act has always required surplus Social Security revenue (revenue in excess of the program's expenditures) to be invested in U.S. government securities (or U.S. government- backed securities). In recent years, however, attention has been focused on alternative investment practices in an effort to increase the interest earnings of the trust funds, among other goals. This chapter explains trust fund investment practices under current law.

BACKGROUND

Social Security is financed primarily by payroll and self-employment taxes, as well as by a portion of the proceeds from the income taxation of Social Security benefits. The revenue is deposited in the U.S. Treasury. Social Security benefits and administrative expenses also are paid from the U.S. Treasury. By law, if Social Security revenue exceeds expenditures, the "surplus" is credited to the Social Security trust funds in the form of U.S. government securities. The money itself, however, is used to pay for whatever other expenses the government may have at the time. There is no separate pool of money set aside for Social Security purposes. That is not to say that the trust funds are ephemeral—as long as the trust funds show a positive balance, they represent the authority and an obligation for the U.S. Treasury to issue benefit checks during periods when the program's expenditures exceed revenue. At the end of calendar year 2008, the trust funds were credited with holdings of $2.4 trillion.[1] By the end of calendar year 2015, trust fund assets are projected to reach $3.0 trillion (in constant 2009 dollars).[2] Section 201 of the Social Security Act provides the following guidelines for trust fund investment:

(1) Funds not immediately in demand for benefits or administrative expenses are to be invested in interest-bearing obligations guaranteed as to both principal and interest by the United States.[3]
(2) Obligations are to be purchased at issue at the issue price or at the market price for outstanding obligations.
(3) The Managing Trustee of the Social Security trust funds (the Secretary of the Treasury) is required to invest in special "nonmarketable" federal public-debt obligations—special issues to the trust funds that are not available to the general public—except where he or she determines that the purchase of marketable federal securities is "in the public interest."
(4) Special issues shall have maturities fixed with due regard for the needs of the trust funds and will pay a rate of interest, calculated at the time of issue, equal to the average market yield on all marketable interest-bearing obligations of the United States that are not due or callable (redeemable) for at least four years.
(5) Marketable federal securities purchased by the trust funds may be sold at the market price and special issue obligations may be redeemed at par plus accrued interest (without penalty for redemption before maturity).

The Treasury Department has determined that the purchase of marketable federal securities (i.e., public issues) would be in the public interest only when it might serve to stabilize the market for Treasury issues. Because an "unstable market" would be characterized by falling bond prices, purchases of marketable federal securities at these times would appear to be advantageous for the trust funds. In practice, however, open market purchases have been rare. Although the trust funds have held public issues in the past, the trust funds currently hold special issues only.[4]

The interest earned on these holdings is credited to the trust funds semiannually (on June 30 and December 31), and it is done by issuing additional federal securities to the trust funds. In calendar year 2008, net interest totaled $116.3 billion.[5] The effective annual rate of interest earned on all obligations held by the trust funds in calendar year 2009 was 4.9%.[6] The interest rate earned on special issues purchased by the trust funds in December 2009 was 2.875%.[7]

The maturity dates of newly issued special issues are set by a standardized procedure. Revenue is invested immediately in short-term issues called certificates of indebtedness, which mature on June 30 of each year. On June 30, certificates of indebtedness that have not been redeemed are reinvested in longer-term special issue bonds. The maturities of these bonds range from 1 to 15 years—the goal is to have about one-fifteenth of them mature each year. This means that the average maturity of these long-term bonds is about 7½ years.

ISSUES

Although critics have questioned whether the current investment policy has constrained the earnings of the trust funds, over the years various advisory councils, congressional committees, and other groups generally have endorsed it. It has been justified as a way to ensure safety of principal and stability of interest, and as a way to avoid intrusion into private markets. It also has been regarded as a way to avoid the political influences that would be inherent in investing outside the U.S. government. Generally, the goal espoused has been to place the trust funds in the same position as any long-term investor seeking a safe rate of return by investing in U.S. securities, and neither advantage nor disadvantage the trust funds relative to these investors or other parts of the government.

For most of the program's history, interest income to the trust funds has not been a major factor in program financing. In recent years, however, the increasing role of interest income, as well as interest by some policymakers in preventing annual Social Security surpluses from being used for other government spending purposes, have focused attention on alternative investment practices.[8]

For example, there have been proposals to replace the special issues held by the trust funds with marketable federal securities, as well as proposals to allow surplus Social Security revenue or a portion of trust fund assets to be invested in assets other than U.S. government obligations, including equities.

End Notes

[1] The Social Security program has two separate trust funds—the Old-Age and Survivors Insurance (OASI) trust fund and the Disability Insurance (DI) trust fund. The amounts cited in this chapter are for the OASI and DI trust funds combined. Historical trust fund data are available on the Social Security Administration (SSA) website at *http://www.ssa.gov/OACT/STATS/table4a3.html.*

[2] Projected trust fund assets are shown in The 2009 Annual Report of the Board of Trustees of the Federal Old-Age and Survivors Insurance and Disability Insurance Trust Funds, May 12, 2009, table VI.F7 (intermediate assumptions), available on the SSA website at http://www.ssa.gov/OACT/TR/2009/lr6f7.html.

[3] Although not specifically authorized by the Social Security Act, the Attorney General has ruled that certain federally sponsored agency obligations may be purchased by the trust funds. Such securities include those issued by the Federal National Mortgage Association (Fannie Mae), the Government National Mortgage Association (Ginnie Mae), and other federal credit entities. Currently, the trust funds do not hold such securities.

[4] The DI trust fund held a small amount of public issues until February 15, 2005. At the end of calendar year 2004, public issues represented 0.002% of total investments held by the trust funds. Data on investments held by the trust funds are available on the SSA website at http://www.ssa.gov/OACT/ProgData/investheld.html.

[5] Data on trust fund receipts, including net interest, are available on the SSA website at http://www.ssa.gov/OACT/ STATS/table4a3.html#income.

[6] Data on effective interest rates earned on assets held by the trust funds are available on the SSA website at http://www.ssa.gov/OACT/ProgData/effectiveRates.html.

[7] Data on nominal interest rates earned on special issues purchased by the trust funds are available on the SSA website at http://www.ssa.gov/OACT/ProgData/newIssueRates.html.

[8] In May 2009, the Social Security Board of Trustees projected that the Social Security system would begin running cash flow deficits in calendar year 2016 (under the intermediate assumptions). Similarly, in August 2009, the Congressional Budget Office (CBO) projected that the system would run cash flow deficits in fiscal years 2010 and 2011, and again beginning in FY2016. CBO attributes the emergence of cash flow deficits in FY2010 and FY2011 to reduced payroll tax revenue as a result of the economic downturn, among other factors. For more information on the Trustees' projections, see The 2009 Annual Report of the Board of Trustees of the Federal Old-Age and Survivors Insurance and Federal Disability Insurance Trust Funds, May 12, 2009, available at http://www.ssa.gov/OACT/TR/ 2009/. For more information on the CBO projections, see The Budget and Economic Outlook: An Update, August 2009, available at http://www.cbo.gov/ ftpdocs/105 xx/doc10521/08-25-BudgetUpdate.pdf. In addition, see the CBO supplemental data table at *http://www.cbo.gov/budget/factsheets/2009c/oasdiTrustfund.pdf.*

In: Social Security: Background, Issues and... ISBN: 978-1-61761-469-9
Editors: Jacob T. Álvarez

Chapter 3

SOCIAL SECURITY, SAVING, AND THE ECONOMY

Brian W. Cashell

SUMMARY

One issue that never seems far from the minds of policymakers is Social Security. At the heart of the issue is the large shortfall of projected revenues needed to meet the mounting costs of the system. For the moment, the amount of Social Security tax receipts exceeds the amount of benefits being paid out. The Social Security trustees estimate that, beginning in 2024, the amount of benefits being paid out will exceed tax collections. According to the trustees' best estimate, the trust fund will be exhausted in the year 2037.

Some have argued that because the Social Security trust fund is intended to meet rising future costs of the program, its surplus should not be counted as offsetting official measures of the budget deficit. With regard to current saving, however, it makes no difference whether the surplus is credited to the trust fund or simply seen as financing current federal government outlays (including Social Security benefits). Off-budget surpluses contribute to national saving in exactly the same way as on-budget surpluses do. The additional saving they represent adds to the national saving rate and allows current investment spending to be higher than it would otherwise be.

With respect to retirement saving, how much is "enough" may be a subjective matter. One standard might be whether accumulated wealth is sufficient to avoid a decline in living standards upon retirement. A number of studies have found that Americans may tend not to save enough to avoid such a decline in their living standard.

Social Security may affect saving in several ways. It may reduce household saving as participants pay some of their Social Security contributions by reducing what they otherwise would have saved on their own. It reduces the risk associated with retirement planning and so may free participants to cut precautionary saving. It may, however, encourage additional saving by making it possible to retire earlier, thus giving participants a longer period of retirement to plan for. To the extent that Social Security involves a transfer of income from workers to retirees, it tends to reduce aggregate household saving by shifting resources from potentially high savers to those who save less.

Proposed reforms have different effects on saving. Those that would move toward a more fully funded system would be likely to increase national saving, investment, and the size of the economy in the future. Reforms that would partially "privatize" using individual accounts, might tend to reduce national saving, unless contributions to those accounts were mandatory. Those that invested Social Security funds in private sector assets would be unlikely to have any effect on national saving.

INTRODUCTION

One issue of perennial concern to policymakers is Social Security. The heart of the issue is that beginning in about 2024, revenues are projected to fall short of benefits. Taxes on those currently in the workforce are credited to the trust fund and benefits to retirees are debited from the trust fund. The balance of the fund itself consists of Treasury securities.

At the moment, the amount of tax receipts exceeds the amount of benefits being paid out, and so the balance in the trust fund is growing. The current "best estimate" of the Social Security trustees is that beginning in 2024, the amount of benefits being paid out will exceed tax collections. At that time, the trust fund will have a balance of $4.3 trillion credited to it, but thereafter it will begin to decline. According to the trustees' most recent best estimate, the trust fund will be exhausted in the year 2037.[1]

Because benefits are projected to exceed receipts in 2024, there is concern among many policymakers that changes need to be made sooner rather than later. If steps are not taken soon, it is argued, much more drastic changes will be needed down the road.

The major function of Social Security is to provide a base upon which to secure the income of the retired population. It does so by transferring income from the working population to those who are no longer in the labor force because of retirement or disability. This is also known as an intergenerational compact, by which those currently working support the retired population with the expectation that future workers will, in turn, provide for their retirement benefits. It also serves a social welfare function, by paying relatively more to retirees who were low-income earners, and survivors and dependents.

From a macroeconomic perspective, however, what matters is the effect on national saving. In a general sense, the economy is blind to the sources of saving. What matters is that saving, whether from the household, business, or public sector is channeled into investments which add to the capital stock, and raise productivity and economic growth.

If individuals set aside substantial amounts during their working lives then the accumulated wealth and their expected Social Security benefits may be sufficient to provide for their retirement years. The more individuals save for their retirement, the higher their standard of living will be when they retire. If individuals are not saving enough to provide for some minimal standard of living in retirement, then increased saving in the public sector is one way to increase national resources from which to fund retirement benefits in the future. The larger the economy, the better able the nation will be to ensure a given minimum standard of living to all retirees.[2]

This paper examines the determinants of household saving and how household saving may be affected by Social Security. The potential effects of possible changes in Social Security on household and national saving are also discussed.[3]

Saving and the Economy

By definition, saving is that proportion of income that is not consumed. Rather, it is made available to sustain and increase the stock of productive capital. The more capital there is available to the workforce, the greater the production of goods and services will be. Combined with labor and technological advances, it is this capital that contributes to the production of all the goods and services that make up national output.

By saving more now, people will be able to consume more in the future. From a macroeconomic perspective, the origin of saving is largely irrelevant. In terms of the collective resources of the nation, a dollar of saving means a dollar of investment whether it is household, business, or public sector saving.

The measure that matters with respect to the federal government's saving is the unified budget. For some purposes, the budget is divided into two accounts; one is referred to as "on-budget" and the other is "off-budget." The so-called off-budget surplus consists almost entirely of Social Security receipts and outlays.[4]

Some have argued that Social Security should not be counted as contributing to official measures of the budget surplus. Keeping Social Security off budget is a procedural device by which Congress signals that the Social Security program should be insulated from other operations of the budget. "Lockbox" proposals would go further in an attempt to deter the current and future Congresses from using Social Security surpluses to justify spending increases for other federal programs or for tax cuts.[5]

With regard to current saving, however, it makes no difference whether those revenues are credited to the trust fund or simply seen as financing current federal government outlays (including Social Security benefits).[6] Without the excess revenues from Social Security taxes, the deficit would be larger, and the federal government's requirements for a share of the national savings pool would be larger as well. Off-budget surpluses contribute to national saving in exactly the same way that an on-budget surplus would. The additional saving they represent adds to the national saving rate and allows current investment spending to be higher than it would otherwise be.

Explaining Household Saving

Any examination of Social Security and its effects on households must begin with an explanation of household saving behavior. What do households take into account when deciding whether, and how much, to save?

Life Cycle Saving

Most economists analyze household saving behavior using what is known as the life-cycle model of consumer behavior. The life-cycle model begins with the basic assumption that most individuals are not myopic but rather take their expected lifetimes into account when deciding how much out of current income to save and how much to spend.

The life-cycle model assumes that individuals seek to avoid large fluctuations in their standard of living over the course of their lifetimes. The model further takes as a given that individuals' incomes tend to follow a predictable pattern over the course of their lifetimes. Typically, that would mean relatively low levels of income during the initial years of work, increases in income up to retirement, and then a drop in income during retirement.

If consumption followed the same pattern as income, it would make for substantial changes in living standards over the course of a lifetime. Instead, consumers are presumed to vary the rate at which they save out of income in order to dampen the effect of changes in income on consumption. Thus, the typical pattern would be that individuals save relatively little in the early stages of their working lives. Then, during peak earning years, saving rates tend to be higher in order to accumulate wealth off of which to live during retirement, when saving tends to fall off considerably.[7]

Precautionary Saving

There is a second consideration that may motivate household saving in addition to retirement. While there may be a typical pattern to incomes, on average, over lifetimes, there is also a certain amount of uncertainty associated with an individual's income at a given time in the future. For example, some incomes vary over the course of the business cycle, and from time to time people may also experience episodes of either voluntary or involuntary unemployment. Thus, in addition to serving as a buffer against lifetime income fluctuations, some fraction of saving may also act to insure against the risks of shorter-term fluctuations in income. This kind of saving may also help to insure against whatever risk might be associated with an individual's pension plan. It is generally referred to as precautionary saving.

Although this may not account for all the possible incentives households have to save, it is enough of a framework to make some general observations about household saving behavior. For example, a temporary decline in incomes will not necessarily have an effect on consumer spending, or on an individual's long-term saving rate, since households have already set funds aside for just such a rainy day. But, any unexpected change in prospects that are likely to extend over an entire lifetime might well affect saving behavior.

Recent Trends in Household Saving

Social Security was created to help secure the economic condition of the retired population by forcing them to save more now in exchange for expected future benefits. Concern remains, however, that many are still not setting aside enough on their own in order to provide adequately for retirement.[8]

It has often been noted that Americans save less than they used to, and that they save less than most other industrialized nations. Those concerns were part of the motivation for the policies that contributed to the elimination of the federal budget deficit briefly in the late 1 990s.[9] Personal saving, as measured in the standard economic accounts, fell steadily between the early 1 980s and 2008. Since April 2008, however, there have been signs of a resurgence in personal saving. Figure 1 shows personal saving as a percentage of aftertax personal income since 1970.

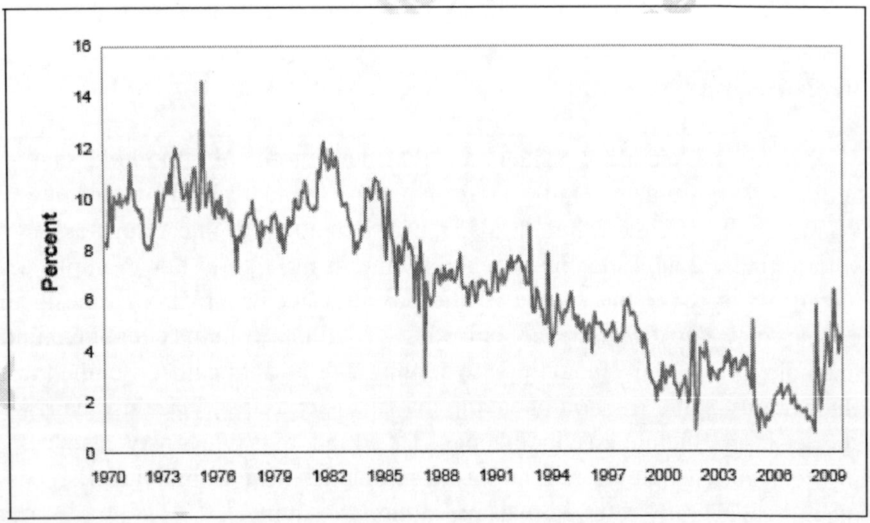

Source: Department of Commerce, Bureau of Economic Analysis.

Figure 1. Personal Saving as a Percentage of Aftertax Personal Income

This measure of saving may give an exaggerated picture of the drop in saving. One of the most marked characteristics of the economy during much of the 1990s was a dramatic rise in equity prices. But, capital gains are not included in the measure of saving shown in Figure 1. A measure of saving based on changes in household net worth would tell a different story. In fact, much of the decline in measured savings, at least through 1999, may have been due to a large increase in equity prices. Between 1990 and 1999, total household net worth more than doubled, while the ratio of household net worth to aftertax income rose from 483% to 630%. [10] The increase in wealth resulting from the rise in equity prices may have led some to feel they did not need to save as much.[11]

Between 1999 and 2003, however, equity prices fell by about one-third, and during that period, the saving rate continued to decline. That household saving continued to be anemic even after the stock market cooled suggests that there are other factors that need to be considered. One candidate would seem to have been the boom in the housing market. Between the start of 1997 and the start of 2007, the house price index published by the Federal Housing Financing Agency (FHFA) increased by nearly 90%.

A number of studies have suggested that housing price appreciation may also have had a significant effect on household saving. Belsky and Prakken, for example, found that in the long run, the effects on household saving of house and equity price variations were similar.[12] They also found that house price appreciation had a more immediate effect and that the effect of equity price appreciation took longer to be fully reflected in the saving rate. The authors suggested that may be because historically equity prices have been more volatile than house prices, and so households may have been more confident in the durability of house price gains. The authors also indicated that the strong effect of the post-2000 boom in house prices may have been partly due to the simultaneous decline in interest rates, which encouraged homeowners to refinance as well as borrow. They left open the question of whether, in other circumstances, house price appreciation would have the same effect on household saving.[13]

After peaking in early 2007, house prices fell significantly. Between April 2007 and September 2009, the FHFA house price index fell by 11%. Equity prices have also come down. Stock prices reached a peak in mid-2007. Between May 2007 and February 2009, the S&P500 stock price index fell by more than 50%. The combined drop in asset prices had a significant effect on household balance sheets. Between the second quarter of 2007 and the first quarter of 2009, total household net worth fell by over $15 trillion, a drop of nearly 24%. Other things being equal, that might be expected to prompt households to cut spending and to save more out of current income to offset the decline in wealth. But with current income falling, it might also seem to be the proverbial rainy day when an increased share of consumption would be financed by reducing saving or drawing on existing wealth.

With respect to household saving, how much is "enough" may be a subjective matter. One standard might be whether accumulated wealth is sufficient to avoid a decline in living standards upon retirement. The life cycle model discussed above assumes that individuals seek to avoid substantial ups and downs in consumption over the course of a lifetime. It might be assumed, then, that the goal of retirement saving is to avoid a significant drop in living standards after retirement.

A number of studies have found, however, that Americans may not save enough to avoid such a decline in their living standard. One, by Hamermesh, of consumption patterns over time found that accumulated wealth, both private and through Social Security, was not sufficient to sustain consumption in early retirement. This study found that, typically, households gradually reduced their consumption spending within several years of having retired. [14]

Bernheim and Scholz, also found that Americans were not saving enough to prepare for retirement.[15] In particular, they found a distinct difference in saving behavior between those with a college education and the rest of the population. In general, those households with a college education were found to have saved enough to avoid a substantial cutback in consumption on retiring, whereas those with less than a college education had not.[16]

In a separate study of household saving behavior, Bernheim concluded that the typical baby- boom household was saving at about one-third thc rate at which they would need to save in order to continue to maintain their current standard of living into retirement. [17]

Engen, Gale, and Uccello make several interesting points regarding the adequacy of household saving for retirement. First, they point out that the ups and downs of the stock market may have little effect on many of those households that are not saving enough, since the ownership of financial assets is heavily concentrated among those households likely to already be saving enough. Second, with regard to what level of saving is considered adequate, it is important to consider the large increase in the consumption of leisure when comparing consumption before and after retirement. Those studies that do not account for the value of leisure time may overestimate the extent of any decline in post-retirement consumption.[18]

Economists at the Center for Retirement Research at Boston College have constructed an index that estimates how many Americans are at risk of experiencing a decline in their living standard at retirement. [19] They found that in 2009, half of households would be "at risk" of a lower standard of living in retirement.

SOCIAL SECURITY AND HOUSEHOLD SAVING

Social Security was intended to provide a base upon which to secure the income of the retired population. As such, it might have been expected to increase the national rate of saving by adding to what households were already setting aside.

However, there is an important question as to whether or not Social Security is a close substitute for personal saving. If it is, Social Security may lead individuals to save less than they would have in its absence.

Consider the stereotypical saver described by the life cycle model discussed above. How would the introduction of a program which required workers to contribute to a retirement fund for their own eventual benefit affect their saving behavior? Whether and how much individual savings are affected by the introduction of such a program would likely depend on the specific features of the program. Suppose that the contributions yielded the same return as other forms of financial assets households might otherwise buy with their saving. In that case, it might be reasonable to expect that individuals would be indifferent between either saving directly or via the contributions to their retirement fund. The introduction of such a program might simply cause individuals to reduce other saving to offset the amount of their contribution.

Suppose, however, that when the program is introduced, retirement benefits are immediately available to everyone who is qualified. This would be closer to a pay-as-you-go system. In this case, those who were very near retirement would contribute relatively little to the program while still receiving the full stream of benefits in retirement. Because those who immediately receive benefits would have contributed little to the program there would be a significant transfer of income from those still working to those in retirement.

Of these two groups, workers tend to save more than do those who are retired. The transfer of income from relatively high savers to relatively low savers would tend to bring down the overall household saving rate. In a strictly pay-as-you-go pension system there would be no offsetting saving on the part of the public sector; all of the contributions would be distributed. Thus, the introduction of a pure pay-as-you-go Social Security system would tend to reduce the national saving rate.

Another way in which Social Security might influence saving was suggested by economist Martin Feldstein. Feldstein argued that Social Security, or any pension for that matter, might lead people to retire sooner than they otherwise would have. For one thing, once covered workers become eligible for an annuity, their pay effectively drops by the amount of the annuity, since they are only working for the difference between their earnings and what their annuity would be.

In an effort to measure the effect of Social Security on saving, Feldstein examined the effect of Social Security wealth on personal saving using data from 1930 to 1992. Social Security wealth was defined as the discounted present value of promised Social Security benefits. Feldstein found that, for each dollar increase in Social Security wealth, personal savings fell by two or three cents.[20] Other studies on the effect of changes in wealth on household saving have found that for each dollar increase in household wealth, saving out of current income falls by somewhere between 1 cent and 7 cents.

If Social Security encourages workers to retire early, then there is a longer period of retirement to save for. But, workers anticipating an earlier retirement might tend to save more on their own. That aspect of Social Security might then tend to raise the personal saving rate. There are two potentially offsetting effects—Social Security substituting for personal saving, and encouraging longer retirement. The first effect tends to reduce personal saving, the second tends to raise it.

Social Security may also affect the precautionary motive for saving. Social Security, as it now stands, is a defined benefit program. In other words, retirement benefits, although they are based on career earnings, are fixed in real terms upon retirement. After that, they do not vary and continue as long as the beneficiary survives. In contrast, were individuals to provide entirely for their own retirement, there would be several sources of risk. For example, there would be uncertainty regarding how long a period of retirement would have to provided for, and there would be some risk associated with those investments which make up individuals' nest eggs.

Thus, Social Security may affect saving in several ways. It may reduce household saving as participants pay some of their Social Security contributions by reducing what they otherwise would have set aside in other investments. It reduces the risk associated with retirement planning and so may free participants to cut precautionary saving. It may also encourage additional saving by making it possible to retire earlier thus providing participants a longer period of retirement to plan for. To the extent that Social Security involves a transfer of income from workers to retirees, it tends to reduce total saving by shifting resources from high savers to relatively low savers.

SAVING AND SOCIAL SECURITY REFORM

As it now stands, Social Security is partially funded. In 2024, benefit payments are projected to exceed tax receipts and, if that happens, will have to be funded out of general revenues. Because of that, some policymakers urged that changes need to be made. The argument is that whatever costs there are to assuring future benefit payments and boosting the confidence of participants in the program will be more easily borne if they are spread out over a long period of time rather than put off until some inevitable day of reckoning.[21]

In the long run, from a national perspective, what matters is how much people save now. Whether it is household saving, business saving, or a federal budget surplus, increased saving means increased investment, a larger capital stock, and higher future living standards. The more that is saved now, the larger the economy will be in the future. If Social Security is changed, those changes could affect saving in one way or another. Using the basic model of life-cycle and precautionary saving explained above it is possible to make a few relevant observations about the potential effects of various kinds of Social Security reform proposals on saving.[22]

There are two broad kinds of reform possibilities that have been most discussed. One is a shift towards a fully-funded plan. The second is a switch from the *defined benefits* that currently characterize Social Security to one that is at least partly a *defined contribution* plan with variable benefits. This second kind of proposal includes some of the suggestions that would privatize some or all of the Social Security program. Another proposal that has been advanced would have some of the trust fund invested in private securities such as corporate stock.

Fully Funded vs. Pay As You Go

If Social Security were fully funded, that would mean that each generation contributed enough to fully provide for their benefits on retirement, and there would be no intergenerational transfers. A pure pay-as-you-go system, on the other hand, would have no trust fund at all, and all Social Security retirement benefits would be paid for by the current contributions of the working population. In this case there would be a continuing transfer of income between generations. Because Social Security is only partially funded, at some point in the future all benefits will be transfers from the working population to retirees if no changes are made.

Switching to a more fully funded program would necessarily involve some combination of increased contributions and reduced benefits. However, any increase in taxes, or cut in benefits, might be partially offset by a reduction in other forms of household saving. A reduction in benefits could also lead households to save less as they seek to maintain a constant level of consumption given a cut in income. For those still working, a cut in prospective benefits might encourage additional saving.

A shift towards a fully funded system would also tend to reduce the intergenerational redistribution of income. A pure pay-as-you-go system takes income from workers, who tend to be savers, and gives it to retirees who tend to save relatively little. In a fully funded system, workers would finance their own retirement benefits. Shifting from a pay-as-you-go system to a fully funded one might reduce the overall bias against saving which is due to the shift of income from savers to dis-savers[23].

Shifting Social Security closer to a fully funded program might also increase confidence on the part of participants that future benefits would be paid. This might serve to diminish the precautionary incentive to save and tend to reduce household saving.

A shift toward a more fully funded system might lead to a reduction in measured household saving, but it is unlikely that the reduction in household saving would offset the increase in public sector saving. The net result is that such a shift would be likely to raise the national saving rate.

Defined Benefit vs. Defined Contribution

Other proposals for Social Security reform involve at least a partial shift from a *defined benefit* plan to a *defined contribution* plan. A defined benefit plan is one where the benefits are set in advance, and while participants must contribute, their benefits do not depend on the performance of those assets in which they are invested. Participants in a defined contribution retirement plan contribute a set amount periodically into an account, and their ultimate retirement benefits depend on the return on the investments held in those accounts.

Depending on the existing level of confidence in future benefits, a shift toward a defined contribution plan might involve an increase in the perceived, or actual, risk faced by participants. To some extent, future benefits would depend on the performance of those assets in which contributions were invested. An increase in risk might lead households to save more for precautionary reasons. A switch toward a defined contribution plan might not, however, involve a great increase in perceived risk given the apparent skepticism among those working now as to whether or not they will get their full Social Security benefits on retiring. If the assets in which the defined contributions are invested yield a higher return, participants might have an incentive to reduce other forms of saving.

Switching to a defined contribution plan, or partially privatizing Social Security, would reduce the federal government surplus because money that had been collected as taxes would be invested directly by individuals. The measured household saving rate would go up as households themselves invested those funds which previously had been paid into the Social Security trust fund. If these new contributions were mandatory, there would be no net effect on national saving as the increase in household saving would offset the decrease in federal government saving.

If the defined contributions were not mandatory, however, it is possible that the household saving rate would not rise enough to offset the decline in the federal government saving rate. Many would be likely to spend at least a portion of the reduction in taxes and some, who might not ever plan to retire might spend all of it. Unless the contributions were made mandatory, the net effect of a switch in the direction of a defined contribution plan could reduce the national saving rate.

There could also be some indirect effects on saving. For example, there might be some increase in the risk associated with retirement savings with a switch to a defined contribution plan which could encourage additional precautionary saving.

Investing the Trust Fund in Private Securities

Another reform proposal that has been advanced is that some of the Social Security trust fund, which currently consists exclusively of Treasury securities, be invested in private securities. Such a change would have no effect on national saving.[24]

If the trust fund were to invest in private securities, corporate stock for example, it would have to either sell some of the Treasury securities it now holds or it would buy stocks out of current tax receipts, and the Treasury would have to find another market for any securities it would otherwise issue to the trust fund. In any case, the supply of Treasury securities would increase, their prices would tend to go down, and their yields would tend to go up. At the same time the demand for corporate stock would increase, and the yield on those stocks would tend to fall. Ultimately the public sector would own some private assets, and the private sector would hold a larger proportion of public sector debt. The only change would be in how the public and private sectors invested their money. There is no evidence indicating that households would increase, or reduce, their saving simply as a result of a shift in relative rates of return on selected financial assets.

If trust fund assets were invested in private sector securities, which yielded a higher rate of return, the trust fund might be made better off. But the improvement in the trust fund would come at the expense of the rest of the federal government budget and those private investors that would otherwise have purchased those assets. The borrowing costs of the federal government would rise because of the increased supply of government securities. The income from capital of other private investors would fall because the increase in demand for private sector securities would be likely to reduce their rate of return.[25]

If individual accounts were created out of trust fund assets and those accounts were invested in private securities the situation would be similar. If Social Security funds were held in personal accounts and invested in private securities, their yield would likely be higher than if they were invested in government securities. But, someone would have to buy the assets that would otherwise have been purchased by the trust fund. And those who did would experience a drop in income from capital.

None of this is to say that investing the trust fund in private securities is undesirable, or would have no effect. Rather, it is to say that such a change would be unlikely to affect the national saving rate.

Social Security will never function exactly like a collective retirement plan where each individual sets aside a given amount in order to provide for his own retirement. Even with a fully funded plan, there will be income transfers among participants. For example, those who live longer than average will gain at the expense of those who die prematurely. As long as the plan is less than fully funded, there will be an ongoing transfer from the working population to those who are already retired.

In the case of individuals, how much they set aside during their working years will determine how well they live in retirement. Similarly, for the nation as a whole, how much people save now will play a role in the size of the economy in the future. The collective saving of households, business, and the public sector will determine how much is invested. The more people invest, the larger a stock of capital people will have and the more productive the labor force will be. A more productive labor force means higher standards of living in the future.

By saving more now, the economy in the future will be larger than it otherwise would be. The larger the economy is and the higher incomes are will make it easier to afford paying retirement benefits no matter how they are financed.

End Notes

[1] The trustees publish three estimates using different assumptions about costs. They call the intermediate projection their "best estimate." This refers to both Old-Age and Survivors Insurance (OASI) and Disability Insurance (DI), which collectively are referred to as OASDI. See the 2008 OASDI trustee's report, at http://www.ssa.gov/OACT/TR/2009/index.html

[2] A larger economy will make it relatively easier to provide retirement benefits. In dealing with the long-range Social Security funding problem, for example, a larger economy would ease any actions needed to fully fund benefit obligations. Increasing federal government saving now would reduce outstanding federal debt, and reduce outlays now devoted to financing the existing public sector debt.

[3] For a more comprehensive discussion of Social Security reform proposals, see CRS Report RL3 1498, *Social Security Reform: Economic Issues*, by Jane G. Gravelle and Marc Labonte.

[4] The Postal Service is also included in the off-budget account.

[5] Some proponents of accounting devices that isolate Social Security from the rest of the budget claim that this would result in greater government saving. This assumes that spending and tax policy decisions depend on what happens to the trust fund.

[6] Neither would it matter with respect to Social Security deficits, currently projected to begin in 2024.

[7] People with higher incomes tend to save more than those with lower incomes; not necessarily just because their incomes are higher, but also because they are more likely to be in their peak earning years.

[8] Social Security is not the only source of retirement income. In fact, in the national income and product accounts published by the Department of Commerce, contributions to Social Security are not counted as part of household saving.

[9] Such as the omnibus Budget Reconciliation Act of 1993, which included both tax increases and spending cuts. See Alberto Alesina, "The Political Economy of the Budget Surplus in the United States," *Journal of Economic Perspectives*, vol.14, no. 3, Summer 2000.

[10] Figures are from the Board of Governors of the Federal Reserve System.

[11] See CRS Report RL33 168, *Why is the Household Saving Rate So Low?*, by Brian W. Cashell.

[12] Eric Belsky and Joel Prakken, "Housing's Impact on Wealth Accumulation, Wealth Distribution and Consumer Spending," National Association of Realtors National Center for Real Estate Research, 2004.

[13] Whether or not house price appreciation might substitute for other forms of saving may depend on if there is a strong bequest motive for saving. Those who save in order to leave a bequest to their children may desire to leave a larger bequest if their children are expected to face higher house prices.

[14] Daniel S. Hamermesh, Consumption During Retirement: The Missing Link in the Life Cycle, *The Review of Economics and Statistics*, vol. LXVI, no. 1, Feb. 1984.

[15] B. Douglas Bernheim and John Karl Scholz, "Do Americans Save Too Little?," Federal Reserve Bank of Philadelphia *Business Review*, Sept.-Oct. 1993.

[16] Income and education tend to be correlated, as are saving and income. Nonetheless, Bernheim and Scholz suggest that one reason some save less than others is that they may not be fully aware of the importance of saving, and that education might be effective in encouraging them to save more.

[17] American Council for Capital Formation, Center for Policy Research, *Special Report*, "Do Households Appreciate Their Financial Vulnerabilities? An Analysis of Actions, Perceptions, and Public Policy," Aug. 1994.

[18] Eric M. Engen, William G. Gale, and Cori Uccello, *Are Households Saving Adequately for Retirement? A Progress Report on Three Projects*, paper presented at the third annual conference of the Retirement Research Consortium, May 2001, p. 19.

[19] Alicia H. Munnell, Anthony Webb, and Francesca Golub-Sass, *The National Retirement Risk Index: After the Crash*, Center for Retirement Research at Boston College, Oct. 2009, available on the web at http://crr.bc.edu/images/stories/ Briefs/ib_9-22.pdf.

[20] Martin Feldstein, "Social Security and Saving: New Time Series Evidence," *National Tax Journal*, June 1996, vol. 49, no. 2.

[21] In principle, the Social Security trust fund represents the obligation of the federal government to pay future benefits. In practice, in an economic sense, it is current Social Security receipts and outlays that matter.

[22] See Eric M. Engen and William G. Gale, "Effects of Social Security Reform on Private and National Saving," in *Social Security Reform: Links to Saving, Investment, and Growth*, Federal Reserve Bank of Boston, Conference Series No. 41. June, 1997.

[23] Dis-savers have a negative saving rate.

[24] Under current rules, if the trust fund purchased private sector securities, those expenditures would be counted as outlays in the unified budget. The increase in measured outlays would reduce the unified budget surplus. But, federal government saving would not change. The Congressional Budget Office is considering changing they way they count purchases of private securities in the budget to eliminate this inconsistency. Whether budget policy depends in any way on particular accounting practices is an issue beyond the scope of this paper. For a discussion, see Congressional Budget Office, Cost Estimate H.R. 4844, Railroad Retirement and Survivors' Improvement Act of 2000.

[25] That is, unless the yields on government bonds had to rise so much, and the yields on the private securities purchased by the trust fund had to fall so much to allow the markets to clear that the shift resulted in no change in capital income to either the private sector or the trust fund.

In: Social Security: Background, Issues and... ISBN: 978-1-61761-469-9
Editors: Jacob T. Álvarez

Chapter 4

SOCIAL SECURITY RETIREMENT EARNINGS TEST: HOW EARNINGS AFFECT BENEFITS

Dawn Nuschler and Alison M. Shelton

SUMMARY

Under the Social Security Retirement Earnings Test (RET), the monthly benefit of a Social Security beneficiary who is below full retirement age (FRA) is reduced if he or she has earnings that exceed an annual threshold. In 2010, a beneficiary who is below FRA and will not attain FRA during the year is subject to a \$1 reduction in benefits for each \$2 of earnings above \$14,160. A beneficiary who will attain FRA in 2010 is subject to a \$1 reduction in benefits for each \$3 of earnings above \$37,680. The annual exempt amounts (\$14,160 and \$37,680 in 2010) generally are adjusted each year according to average wage growth.

If a beneficiary is affected by the RET, his or her monthly benefit may be reduced in part or in full, depending on the total applicable reduction. For example, if the total applicable reduction is greater than the beneficiary's monthly benefit amount, no monthly benefit is payable for one or more months. If family members also receive auxiliary benefits based on the beneficiary's work record, the reduction is pro-rated and applied to all benefits payable on that work record (including benefits paid to spouses who are *above* FRA). For example, in the case of a family consisting of a worker beneficiary who has earnings above the annual exempt amount and a spouse and child who receive benefits based on his or her work record, the benefit reduction that applies under the RET is charged against the total family benefit.

The RET has been part of the Social Security program in some form throughout the program's history. The original rationale for the RET was that, as a social insurance system, Social Security protects workers from certain risks, including the loss of earnings due to retirement. Therefore, benefits should be withheld from workers who show by their earnings that they have not "retired." The RET does not apply to Social Security disability beneficiaries who are subject to separate limitations on earnings.

If a beneficiary is affected by the RET, his or her monthly benefit is *recomputed,* and the dollar amount of the monthly benefit is *increased,* when he or she attains FRA. This feature of the RET, which allows beneficiaries to recoup benefits "lost" as a result of the RET, is not widely known or understood. The benefit recomputation at FRA is done by adjusting (lessening) the actuarial reduction for retirement before FRA that was applied in the initial benefit computation to take into account months for which benefits were reduced in part or in full under the RET. Any spousal benefits that were reduced because of the RET are recomputed when the spouse attains FRA. For a spouse who has already attained FRA, however, there is no subsequent adjustment to benefits to take into account months for which no benefit or a partial benefit was paid as a result of the RET.

The Social Security Administration estimates that elimination of the RET for individuals aged 62 or older would have a negative effect on the Social Security trust fund in the amount of $81 billion from 2012 to 2018, although it would have no major effect on Social Security's projected long-range financial outlook.

This chapter explains how the RET works under current law. In addition, it provides benefit examples to illustrate the effect of the RET on Social Security beneficiaries who are below FRA and family members who receive benefits based on their work records. It also briefly discusses policy issues, including recent research on the effect of the RET on work effort and the decision to claim Social Security benefits.

INTRODUCTION

Social Security benefits received before a person attains full retirement age (FRA)[1] are subject to an actuarial reduction for early retirement and also may be reduced by the Social Security Retirement Earnings Test (RET) if the beneficiary has earnings that exceed an annual threshold. Under the RET, a beneficiary who is below FRA and will not attain FRA during the calendar year is subject to a $1 reduction in benefits for each $2 of earnings above an annual exempt amount, which is $14,160 in 2010. During the calendar year in which a beneficiary attains FRA, he or she is subject to a $1 reduction in benefits for each $3 of earnings above a higher annual exempt amount, which is $37,680 in 2010.[2]

This chapter explains how the RET is applied under current law and provides detailed benefit examples to show how the RET affects both the worker beneficiary and any family members (auxiliary beneficiaries) who receive benefits based on the worker beneficiary's record. The report points out features of the RET that are not widely known or understood, such as the recomputation of benefits when a beneficiary attains FRA to adjust (increase) benefits to take into account months for which no benefit or a partial benefit was paid as a result of the RET. Finally, the report discusses policy issues related to the RET, including recent research on the effect of the RET on work effort and the decision to claim Social Security benefits.

Key points discussed in the report include the following:

- Benefits may be reduced in part or in full for one or more months as a result of the RET.
- Benefit reductions under the RET apply both to the worker beneficiary and to any family members (auxiliary beneficiaries) who receive benefits based on the worker beneficiary's record. This would include, for example, a dependent child and a spouse who may have already attained FRA.
- When a worker beneficiary and family members are subject to a benefit reduction under the RET, the reduction is pro-rated and applied to each person's benefit in proportion to each person's original entitlement amount. (The total amount of the reduction remains the same, but the reduction is pro-rated across more people.)
- An auxiliary beneficiary may be subject to a reduction in benefits under the RET both on the basis of the worker beneficiary's earnings

above the exempt amount and on the basis of his or her own earnings above the exempt amount.

- Benefits "lost" as a result of the RET may be recouped by the beneficiary. When a beneficiary attains FRA and is no longer subject to the RET, his or her benefits are adjusted upward to take into account months for which no benefit or a partial benefit was paid as a result of the RET.
- The Social Security Administration (SSA) estimates that elimination of the RET for individuals aged 62 or older would have no major effect on Social Security's projected long-range financial outlook. In the short run, however, SSA estimates that eliminating the RET would have a negative effect on the Social Security trust fund in the amount of $81 billion from 2012 to 2018.
- The RET raises several policy issues, including the effect of the RET on labor supply (how many hours to work and when to retire) and its effect on when workers claim Social Security benefits.

Historical Background

In general, Social Security benefits are meant to replace, in part, earnings lost to an individual or family because of retirement, disability, or death. The rationale for the RET was outlined in the 1935 report of the Committee on Economic Security, which recommended that no benefits be paid before a person had "retired from gainful employment."[3]

The original Social Security Act barred payment of benefits for any month in which a beneficiary received wages from "regular employment."[4] This provision never went into effect, however, because the Social Security Board and many other analysts thought it would be nearly impossible to determine what was "regular" employment in different industries and occupations. Instead, the board recommended a specific monetary amount to simplify administration. In 1939, Congress incorporated these recommendations in amendments to the Social Security Act.[5] Starting with the first benefits paid in 1940, benefits were withheld only for months in which covered earnings were $15 or more.

The RET has evolved from a monthly test to an annual one (with the exception of the "grace year" as discussed below) and from a provision that initially affected all worker beneficiaries to one that affects beneficiaries who are below the FRA. The most recent legislative change to the RET was in 2000 when Congress eliminated the RET for beneficiaries beginning with the month they attain FRA. This change was made under the Senior Citizens Freedom to Work Act (P.L. 106-182). Before the change in 2000, the RET applied to beneficiaries until they attained the age of 70.

CURRENT LAW

Social Security Worker and Auxiliary Benefits

Social Security benefits are based on the average of a worker's highest 35 years of earnings. A worker's primary insurance amount (PIA) is computed by applying the Social Security benefit formula to the worker's career-average, wage-indexed earnings. The benefit formula replaces a higher percentage of the pre-retirement earnings of workers with low career-average earnings than for workers with high career-average earnings.

A worker's initial monthly benefit is equal to the worker's PIA if he or she begins receiving benefits at FRA. A worker's initial monthly benefit will be *less* than his or her PIA if the worker begins receiving benefits *before* FRA, and it will be *greater* than his or her PIA if the worker begins receiving benefits *after* FRA.[6] For a more detailed explanation of the Social Security benefit computation and the actuarial adjustment to benefits claimed before or after FRA, see Appendix A.

Social Security also provides auxiliary benefits to eligible family members of a retired, disabled or deceased worker. Benefits payable to family members are equal to a specified percentage of the worker's PIA. For example, a spouse's benefit is equal to 50% of the worker's PIA, and a widow(er) 's benefit is equal to 100% of the deceased worker's PIA. The total amount of benefits payable to a family based on a retired or deceased worker's record is capped by the maximum family benefit amount, which varies from 150% to 188% of the retired or deceased worker's PIA. For more information on auxiliary benefits and the maximum family benefit amount, see Appendix B.

The RET Applies to Beneficiaries below the Social Security Full Retirement Age

The RET applies to beneficiaries who are below the Social Security FRA and have earnings that exceed a specified dollar amount (an annual exempt amount). The RET does not apply to worker beneficiaries who are at or above FRA (the RET no longer applies beginning with the month the beneficiary attains FRA) or to those who are disabled.[7] In addition, the RET does not apply to beneficiaries living outside the United States whose work is not covered by the U.S Social Security system; in this case, the "foreign work test" is applied. Self-employed persons are subject to the RET if they have performed "substantial services," which are determined by the nature of the service performed rather than by profit or loss.

The RET Reduces Social Security Benefits

For beneficiaries who are below FRA and will not attain FRA during the calendar year, Social Security benefits are reduced by $1 for each $2 earned above the exempt amount. For beneficiaries who will attain FRA during the calendar year, Social Security benefits are reduced by $1 for each $3 earned above the exempt amount.[8]

Earnings above the exempt amount are charged against monthly benefits beginning with the first chargeable month of the year, at the applicable rate of $1 for each $2 or $3 of earnings above the exempt amount, and continue to be charged each month until all earnings above the exempt amount have been charged against the worker's benefits and any benefits payable to family members on his or her work record. A partial benefit is paid when the charge to a given month is less than the monthly benefit.

The RET Exempt Amounts

The RET applies only to wage and salary income (i.e., earnings from work). It does not apply to income from pensions, rents, dividends, interest, and other types of "unearned" income.

The RET annual exempt amounts in 2010 are $14,160 for beneficiaries who are below FRA and will not attain FRA in 2010, and $37,680 for beneficiaries who will attain FRA in 2010. The RET exempt amounts generally increase each year at the same rate as average wages in the economy.[9] Appendix C shows the annual exempt amounts under the RET from calendar years 2000 to 2010.

Grace Year

A "grace year" applies during the first year of benefit entitlement (or, for dependent beneficiaries, in the last year of benefit entitlement). During the grace year, the RET is applied effectively on a monthly basis. A beneficiary may receive full benefits for any month during which his or her earnings do not exceed one-twelfth of the annual exempt amount, regardless of the total amount of earnings for the year.

As an example, consider a worker aged 62 who (1) has $60,000 in earnings from January through June 2010, (2) claims Social Security retirement benefits on July 1, 2010, and (3) has no additional earnings for the remainder of the year (July through December 2010). Because this person does not have earnings above the 2010 monthly exempt amount of $1,180 in any month from July through December 2010, full benefits are paid for each month. This is the case even though this person's total earnings for 2010 are $60,000, an amount higher than the 2010 annual exempt amount of $14,160.

The RET May Affect Social Security Benefits Received by Spouses, Survivors and Other Dependents

There are two ways in which a person who receives Social Security auxiliary benefits (benefits paid to spouses, survivors, and other dependents) could be affected by the RET. First, benefits paid to spouses and dependents are affected by the RET when the benefits are based on the record of a worker beneficiary who is subject to the RET (i.e., the worker beneficiary is below FRA and has earnings above the exempt amount). This includes benefits paid to spouses who are below FRA as well as to those who are *above* FRA. An exception is made for auxiliary benefits paid to divorced spouses. If a divorced spouse has been divorced from the worker beneficiary for at least two years, the auxiliary benefit is not affected by the worker beneficiary's earnings.

Second, benefits paid to spouses (including divorced spouses) and dependents are affected by the RET when the auxiliary beneficiary is below FRA and has his or her own earnings above the exempt amount. Auxiliary beneficiaries are subject to the same annual exempt amounts and benefit reduction rates that apply to worker beneficiaries.

Dually Entitled Beneficiaries

A person receiving spousal benefits who is affected by the RET based on his or her own earnings above the exempt amount may be simultaneously (dually) entitled to a retired-worker benefit based on his or her own work record. A dually entitled beneficiary receives his or her own retired- worker benefit first, plus any spousal benefit remaining after the spousal benefit is reduced based on the retired-worker benefit. In effect, the total benefit payable to a dually entitled beneficiary is capped at the higher of the retired-worker benefit and the spousal benefit.

In the case of a dually entitled beneficiary, his or her own earnings above the exempt amount affect both his or her own retired-worker benefit and the spousal benefit.[10] In addition, if the worker beneficiary on whose record the spousal benefit is based has earnings above the exempt amount, the spousal benefit is affected by those earnings as well. When a dually entitled beneficiary attains FRA, each benefit that was affected by the RET (the retired-worker benefit or the spousal benefit) is adjusted upward to take into account months for which no benefit or a partial benefit was paid as a result of the RET.

An example is provided later in the report to show how benefits paid to a non-working spouse are affected when the worker beneficiary has earnings above the exempt amount. In addition, an example is provided to show how spousal benefits are affected when both the worker beneficiary and the spouse have earnings above the exempt amount.

Benefits Withheld under the RET are Restored Starting at FRA

When a beneficiary has had benefits fully or partially withheld under the RET, benefits "lost" as a result of the RET are restored starting at FRA. Specifically, the worker's benefits are recomputed—and increased—when he or she attains FRA. In the benefit recomputation at FRA, the actuarial reduction for benefit entitlement before FRA that was applied in the initial benefit computation is adjusted (the actuarial reduction for early retirement is lessened) to reflect the number of months the worker received no benefit or a partial benefit as a result of the RET.[11]

In the initial benefit computation, retirement benefits are reduced for early retirement by a fraction of the worker's PIA for each month of entitlement before FRA. Retirement benefits are reduced by five-ninths of 1% (or 0.0056) of the worker's PIA for each of the first 36 months of entitlement before FRA. Stated another way, the actuarial reduction for early retirement is about 6.7% per year for the first three years of entitlement before FRA (i.e., from the age of 62 to 65). For each additional month of entitlement before FRA (up to 24 months), retirement benefits are reduced by five-twelfths of 1% (or 0.0042) of the worker's PIA, for an actuarial reduction of 5% per year (i.e., from the age of 65 to 67).[12]

Stated generally, if a worker's benefits are reduced in the initial benefit computation to reflect *x months* of early retirement, and the worker subsequently has benefits withheld under the RET for *y months*, the benefit recomputation at FRA will reflect an actuarial reduction for (*x minus y) months* of early retirement, resulting in a higher monthly benefit amount starting at FRA.

As an example, consider a worker who starts receiving Social Security retirement benefits at the age of 62, although his or her FRA is 66, and he or she has earnings above the RET exempt amount. Because the person claims retirement benefits four years before attaining FRA and has earnings above the RET threshold, he or she will be subject to both the actuarial reduction for benefit entitlement before FRA and benefit withholding under the RET. The actuarial reduction is equal to about 6.7% per year for the first three years of benefit entitlement before FRA and 5% per year thereafter. In this example, the total actuarial reduction in the person's initial monthly benefit is 25% ((6.7% * 3 years) + (5% * 1 year)). In addition, the person continues to work throughout the four-year period from the age of 62 to 66 and has earnings high enough to cause a reduction in his or her monthly benefit under the RET.[13] If the RET results in a 50% reduction in Social Security benefits in each of the four years from the age of 62 to 66, the person would have benefits withheld for six months each year, for a total of 24 months.[14] The benefit recomputation when the person attains FRA will take into account that the person received no benefits for 24 months as a result of the RET. Specifically, the reduction factor for benefit entitlement before FRA will be adjusted from 48 months to 24 months. Starting at FRA, the person's monthly benefit will be increased to reflect an actuarial reduction for benefit entitlement before FRA of about 13.4% (6.7% * 2 years), instead of 25%. The person receives a higher monthly benefit because benefits withheld under the RET are restored starting at FRA.

If spousal benefits are withheld under the RET (as discussed in section "The RET May Affect Social Security Benefits Received by Spouses, Survivors and Other Dependents"), they will be adjusted upward when the spouse attains FRA (not when the worker beneficiary attains FRA). For a spouse who has already attained FRA, there is no subsequent adjustment to benefits to take into account months for which no benefit or a partial benefit was paid as a result of the RET.

WORKER BENEFICIARIES WITH EARNINGS IN 2006

Table 1 shows the number of worker beneficiaries who had earnings in 2006, the most recent year for which data are available. About 1.3 million worker beneficiaries who were below FRA during all or part of 2006 had earnings.

With respect to the data shown in Table 1, it is important to note that not all worker beneficiaries with earnings are affected by the RET. For example, those who have earnings below the exempt amount are not affected by the RET. In addition, those who are in the first year of entitlement may benefit from the "grace year" provision and are not subject to the RET during any months in which they have earnings that are lower than the monthly RET exempt amount (i.e., the annual RET exempt amount divided by 12).

Table 1. Number of Worker Beneficiaries with Earnings in 2006

Earnings	Below FRA Throughout 2006[a]	Attained FRA in 2006[b]
$1 - 4,999	356,000	117,500
5,000 - 9,999	226,500	69,900
10,000 - 14,999	213,500	60,900
15,000 - 19,999	72,800	35,800
20,000 - 24,999	39,200	17,100
25,000 - 29,999	17,600	9,700
30,000 - 34,999	10,200	7,800

Table 1. (Continued)

Earnings	Below FRA Throughout 2006[a]	Attained FRA in 2006[b]
35,000 - 39,999	6,300	6,000
40,000 - 44,999	5,600	2,100
45,000 - 49,999	3,600	1,700
50,000 - 54,999	2,500	1,500
55,000 - 59,999	2,100	1,300
60,000 - 64,999	1,800	700
65,000 - 69,999	1,300	800
70,000 - 74,999	1,300	500
75,000 - 79,999	1,000	700
80,000 - 84,999	800	600
85,000 - 89,999	900	400
90,000 - 99,999	900	800
100,000 or more	5,400	3,100
Total with Earnings	**969,300**	**338,900**

Sources: Social Security Administration, Office of Research, Evaluation and Statistics: 2007 1 Percent Continuous Work History Sample and 2006 Employee and Employer File. Data provided by the Social Security Administration to the Congressional Research Service on February 24, 2010.

Note: Table includes individuals who were awarded retired-worker benefits by December 2005.

a. The exempt amounts for persons who were below FRA throughout 2006 were $12,480 annually and $1,040 monthly.

b. The exempt amounts for persons who attained FRA in 2006 were $33,240 annually and $2,770 monthly.

APPLICATION OF THE RETIREMENT EARNINGS TEST

Table 2 illustrates the application of the RET to a single person who receives benefits based on his or her own work record. The table illustrates the effect of the RET on single worker beneficiaries in two different age groups, reflecting the application of different annual exempt amounts and benefit reduction rates under the RET for beneficiaries who will remain below FRA throughout the calendar year and beneficiaries who will attain FRA during the calendar year. The two single worker beneficiaries in the examples have the following characteristics:

Table 2. Application of the Retirement Earnings Test to a Single Worker Beneficiary with Earnings Above the Annual Exempt Amount

Step	Worker Beneficiary is Below FRA Throughout Calendar Year	Worker Beneficiary Will Attain FRA During Calendar Year
1. Social Security monthly benefit	$2,000	$2,000
2. Calculation of earnings above annual exempt amount		
Earnings in 2010	$40,000	$40,000
RET exempt amount in 2010	$14,160	$37,680
Earnings above annual exempt amount	$25,840	$2,320
3. RET charge (= one-half of earnings above exempt amount for beneficiary below FRA, or one-third of earnings above exempt amount for beneficiary who will attain FRA during calendar year)	$12,920	$773
4. Application of the RET. The benefit paid each month equals the monthly benefit amount of $2,000 minus the remaining balance of the RET charge. The RET charge for a given month cannot exceed the benefit for that month, but it may reduce the benefit to zero in some months. A partial benefit is paid if the remaining RET balance is less than the monthly benefit amount.		

Table 2. (Continued)

Step	Worker Beneficiary is Below FRAThroughout Calendar Year	Worker Beneficiary Will Attain FRA During Calendar Year
January monthly benefit	$0[a]	$1,227[b]
February through June monthly benefits	$0a	$2,000
July monthly benefit	$1,080[b]	$2,000
August through December monthly benefits: full benefits paid	$2,000	$2,000, plus increase resulting from benefit recomputation at FRA to take into account months for which no benefit or a partial benefit was paid due to the RET

Source: Congressional Research Service.

Notes: In this example, it is assumed that the worker beneficiary receives benefits based on his or her own work record only. The starting benefit amounts are assumed to include reductions for retirement before FRA, and to exclude other reductions that may apply. The example has been constructed so that the year" provision does not apply, by assuming that the beneficiary both works and collects benefits over the full calendar year. (See "Grace Year" section.) Alternatively, under the grace year provision, a beneficiary who is in the first year of entitlement is not subject to the RET in any month during which he or she has earnings that do not exceed the monthly exempt amount (the annual exempt amount divided by 12), regardless of the beneficiary's total amount of earnings for the year.

a. No benefit is paid this month because the beneficiary's RET balance is larger than the monthly benefit amount, so the RET charge for this month is equal to the benefit amount.

b. A partial benefit is paid this month because the beneficiary's RET balance is smaller than the monthly benefit amount.

Single Worker Beneficiary Who is Below FRA Throughout the Calendar Year. This example shows a worker beneficiary with a monthly benefit amount of $2,000 (this amount has already been adjusted for retirement before FRA) and $40,000 of earnings in 2010. Because this worker beneficiary is below FRA throughout the calendar year, he or she is subject to a $1 reduction in benefits for each $2 of earnings above the annual exempt amount of $14,160 in 2010.

Single Worker Beneficiary Who Will Attain FRA During the Calendar Year. This example shows a worker beneficiary with a monthly benefit amount of $2,000 (this amount has already been adjusted for retirement before FRA) and $40,000 of earnings in 2010. Because this worker beneficiary will attain FRA during the calendar year, he or she is subject to a $1 reduction in benefits for each $3 of earnings above the annual exempt amount of $37,680 in 2010.

As discussed above, certain auxiliary benefits (benefits paid to the worker's family members such as a spouse or children) are subject to withholding under the RET if either the worker beneficiary or the auxiliary beneficiary has earnings above the exempt amount. When the worker beneficiary has earnings above the exempt amount, these earnings are charged against the total family benefit, that is, the total of benefits paid to the worker beneficiary and auxiliary beneficiaries who receive benefits based on the worker beneficiary's record. (When the auxiliary beneficiary has earnings above the exempt amount, these earnings are charged only against the auxiliary beneficiary's benefit, as discussed below.)

Table 3 provides an example of a worker beneficiary who is entitled to a monthly retirement benefit of $2,000 (this amount has already been adjusted for retirement before FRA). In addition, the worker beneficiary's spouse and child are each entitled to a monthly auxiliary benefit of $1,000 based on the worker beneficiary's record. Therefore, the total monthly family benefit is $4,000.[15]

If the worker beneficiary is below FRA and has earnings above the exempt amount, reductions under the RET are pro-rated among family members in proportion to each family member's original entitlement amount, before any adjustment for the family maximum or for retirement before FRA.[16] The total amount of the reduction remains the same, but the reduction is pro-rated across more people. If reductions under the RET are large enough to exceed the total family benefit for one or more months, no benefits are payable to the family for those months. If a partial benefit is payable for one month, reflecting a reduction under the RET for that month that is less than the total family benefit, the partial benefit is pro-rated among family members.

In Table 3, benefits for the illustrative family are shown under two phases of the RET. The first case shows a family headed by a worker beneficiary who is below FRA throughout the calendar year and is subject to a benefit reduction under the RET equal to one-half of earnings above the lower exempt amount of $14,160 in 2010. The second case shows a family headed by a worker beneficiary who will attain FRA during the calendar year and is subject to a benefit reduction under the RET equal to one-third of earnings above the higher exempt amount of $37,680 in 2010.

Table 3. Application of the Retirement Earnings Test to a Family Consisting of a Worker Beneficiary with Earnings Above the Annual Exempt Amount and Auxiliary Beneficiaries (a Spouse and a Child)

Step	Worker Beneficiary is Below FRA Throughout Calendar Year	Worker Beneficiary Will Attain FRA During Calendar Year
1. Social Security unreduced total monthly family benefit	$4,000	$4,000
of which:	*of which:*	*of which:*
Worker beneficiary's unreduced benefit	*$2,000*	*$2,000*
Spouse's unreduced benefit	*$1,000*	*$1,000*
Child's unreduced benefit	*$1,000*	*$1,000*
2. Calculation of worker beneficiary's earnings above the annual exempt amount		
Worker beneficiary's earnings in 2010	$40,000	$40,000
RET exempt amount in 2010	$14,160	$37,680
Worker beneficiary's earnings above the annual exempt amount	$25,840	$2,320
3. RET charge (= one-half of earnings above the exempt amount for worker beneficiary who is below FRA, or one-third of earnings above the exempt amount for worker beneficiary who will attain FRA during calendar year)	$12,920	$773
4. Application of the RET to the total family benefit. The total family benefit paid each month equals the monthly family benefit amount of $4,000 minus the remaining balance of the RET charge, where the RET		

Table 3. (Continued)

Step	Worker Beneficiary is Below FRA Throughout Calendar Year	Worker Beneficiary Will Attain FRA During Calendar Year
charge is pro-rated across family members by original benefit amount (shown in notes to the table). The RET charge for a given month cannot exceed the total family benefit for that month, but it may reduce the family benefit to zero in some months. A partial benefit is paid if the remaining RET balance is less than the monthly family benefit amount.		
January total monthly family benefit	$0[a]	$3,227[b]
February and March total monthly family benefit	$0[a]	$4,000
April total monthly family benefit	$3,080[c]	$4,000
May through December total monthly family benefit	$4,000	$4,000, plus increase resulting from benefit recomputation at FRA to take into account months for which no benefit or a partial benefit was paid due to the RET

Source: Congressional Research Service.

Notes: In this example, it is assumed that the worker beneficiary receives benefits based on his or her own work record only, and that the spouse and child beneficiaries receive auxiliary benefits based on the worker beneficiary's record only. The starting benefit amounts are assumed to include reductions for retirement before FRA, and to exclude other benefit reductions that may apply, such as those related to receipt of a non-covered pension and the maximum family benefit amount. The example has been constructed so that the "grace year" provision does not apply, by assuming that the beneficiary both works and collects benefits over the full calendar year. (See "Grace Year" section.) Alternatively, under the grace year provision a beneficiary who is in the first year of entitlement is not subject to the RET in any month during which he or she has earnings that do not exceed the monthly exempt amount (the annual exempt amount divided by 12), regardless of the beneficiary's total amount of earnings for the year.

a. No benefit is paid this month because the beneficiary's RET balance is larger than the monthly benefit amount, so the RET charge for this month is equal to the benefit amount.
b. A partial benefit is paid to each family member in January because the RET balance is smaller than the total family benefit amount for the month. The RET balance of $773 is pro-rated and charged against all beneficiaries in proportion to their original entitlement amounts. One-half of the RET charge ($387) is applied to the worker beneficiary and one-fourth ($193) each is applied to the spouse and child. Therefore the worker beneficiary receives a January benefit of $1,613 ($2,000 - $387) and the spouse and child each receive January benefits of $807 ($1,000 - $193).
c. A partial benefit is paid to each family member in April because the remaining RET balance is smaller than the total family benefit amount for the month. The remaining RET balance of $920 is pro-rated and charged against all beneficiaries in proportion to their original entitlement amounts. One-half of the RET charge ($460) is applied to the worker beneficiary and one-fourth ($230) each is applied to the spouse and child. Therefore the worker beneficiary receives an April benefit of $1,540 ($2,000 - $460) and the spouse and child each receive April benefits of $770 ($1,000 - $230).

The preceding examples illustrate cases in which the worker beneficiary has earnings above the exempt amount. In some cases, both the worker beneficiary and an auxiliary beneficiary (such as a spouse) may have earnings above the exempt amount. Table 4 shows an example of a couple in which (1) one member, the worker beneficiary, receives a retired-worker benefit based on his or her own work record, and (2) one member, the auxiliary beneficiary, receives a spousal benefit only. Both beneficiaries are assumed to be below FRA throughout the calendar year and to have earnings above the RET exempt amount.[17] Because neither beneficiary will attain FRA during the calendar year, both are subject to the same RET exempt amount and benefit reduction rate. Benefit reductions under the RET are applied to the couple in the following order:[18]

- First, the worker beneficiary's RET charge is pro-rated and applied to both the worker beneficiary's retired-worker benefit and the auxiliary beneficiary's spousal benefit.[19]
- Second, if there is a balance remaining on the spousal benefit (if the spousal benefit has not been reduced to zero), the auxiliary beneficiary's RET charge is applied to (and further reduces) his or her spousal benefit only (the auxiliary beneficiary's earnings above the

RET exempt amount do not affect the worker beneficiary's retired-worker benefit).

Table 4. Application of the Retirement Earnings Test to a Couple Consisting of a Worker Beneficiary and an Auxiliary (Spousal) Beneficiary, Both of Whom Have Earnings Above the Annual Exempt Amount and Are Below FRA Throughout the Calendar Year

Step	Spouse #1: Worker Beneficiary	Spouse #2: Auxiliary Beneficiary
1. Social Security retired-worker benefit, based on own work record	$2,000	
2. Social Security auxiliary (spousal) benefit		$1,000
3. Calculation of earnings above annual exempt amount		
Earnings in 2010	$25,000	$25,000
RET exempt amount in 2010	$14,160	$14,160
Earnings above annual exempt amount	$10,840	$10,840
4. RET charge (= one-half of earnings above the exempt amount for both worker beneficiary and auxiliary beneficiary, both of whom are below FRA throughout the calendar year)	$5,420	$5,420
5. Application of the RET		
January benefit: Worker beneficiary's RET charge is applied to total family benefits of $3,000.	$0	$0
February benefit: Balance of worker beneficiary's RET charge ($2,420 = $5,420 -$3,000) is prorated between worker beneficiary and auxiliary beneficiary in proportion to their original entitlement amount (a ratio of two to one): $1,613 is applied to the worker beneficiary and $807 is applied to the auxiliary beneficiary. In addition, $193 of auxiliary	$387	$0

Table 4. (Continued)

Step	Spouse #1: Worker Beneficiary	Spouse #2: Auxiliary Beneficiary
beneficiary's RET charge is applied to the auxiliary beneficiary's benefit only, reducing it to zero.		
March through July monthly benefits: Worker beneficiary receives full monthly benefits. Auxiliary beneficiary's monthly benefit is reduced to zero by his or her own RET charge (worker beneficiary is not affected).	$2,000	$0
August monthly benefit: Worker beneficiary receives full monthly benefit. Auxiliary beneficiary's RET balance of $227 ($5,420 - $5,193) is charged to his or her benefit.	$2,000	$773
September through December monthly benefits: full benefits paid to both spouses	$2,000	$1,000

Source: Congressional Research Service.

Notes: In this example, both beneficiaries are assumed to be below FRA throughout the calendar year and therefore are subject to the same RET exempt amount and benefit reduction rate. It is assumed that the worker beneficiary receives benefits based on his or her own work record only, and that the auxiliary beneficiary (spouse) receives benefits based on the worker beneficiary's record only. The starting benefit amounts are assumed to include reductions for retirement before FRA, and to exclude other benefit reductions that may apply, such as those related to receipt of a non-covered pension. The example has been constructed so that the "grace year" provision does not apply, by assuming that the beneficiaries both work and collect benefits over the full calendar year. (See "Grace Year" section.) Alternatively, under the grace year provision, a beneficiary who is in the first year of entitlement is not subject to the RET in any month during which he or she has earnings that do not exceed the monthly exempt amount (the annual exempt amount divided by 12), regardless of the beneficiary's total amount of earnings for the year.

More complex situations may exist in which, for example, a person is dually entitled to a retired- worker benefit (based on his or her own work record) and a spousal benefit (based on a different work record) and the person has earnings above the exempt amount. In the case of a dually- entitled beneficiary, his or her earnings above the exempt amount affect both his or her own retired-worker benefit and the spousal benefit that he or she receives. The dually entitled beneficiary's earnings above the exempt amount do not affect the retired-worker benefit received by his or her spouse because that benefit is based on the spouse's work record.

Table 5 summarizes the applicability of the RET to worker beneficiaries and auxiliary beneficiaries when either type of beneficiary has earnings above the exempt amount.

Table 5. Applicability of the Retirement Earnings Test to Worker Beneficiaries and Auxiliary Beneficiaries

Beneficiary Type	Worker Beneficiary Has Earnings Above the Exempt Amount	Auxiliary Beneficiary Has Earnings Above the Exempt Amount
Worker Beneficiary	Worker beneficiary's own benefit is reduced.	Only the auxiliary benefit is reduced, not the worker beneficiary's benefit.
Auxiliary Beneficiary: Spouse	Auxiliary benefits to spouses are reduced for the worker beneficiary's earnings above the exempt amount, which are charged against the total family benefit.	Only the auxiliary benefit is reduced, not the worker beneficiary's benefit.
Auxiliary Beneficiary: Divorced Spouse	A divorced spouse's benefit is not reduced for the worker beneficiary's earnings above the exempt amount if the couple has been divorced at least two years.	Only the auxiliary benefit is reduced, not the worker beneficiary's benefit.
Auxiliary Beneficiary: Child	Auxiliary benefits to children are reduced for the worker beneficiary's earnings above the exempt amount, which are charged against the total family benefit.	Only the auxiliary benefit is reduced, not the worker beneficiary's benefit.
Auxiliary Beneficiary: Mother or Father with Qualifying Child in Care (child under age 16 or disabled)	Not applicable (worker beneficiary is deceased).	The mother's or father's benefit is reduced.

Table 5. (Continued)

Beneficiary Type	Worker Beneficiary Has Earnings Above the Exempt Amount	Auxiliary Beneficiary Has Earnings Above the Exempt Amount
Auxiliary Beneficiary: Widow(er)	Not applicable (worker beneficiary is deceased).	The widow(er)'s benefit is reduced.
Auxiliary Beneficiary: Parent	Not applicable (worker beneficiary is deceased).	The parent's benefit is reduced.

Source: Social Security Administration, *Social Security Handbook*, revised November 19, 2007, http://www.ssa.gov/OP_Home/handbook/handbook.18/handbook-1806.html.

Notes: A worker beneficiary's spouse or child who is receiving mother's/father's benefits or child's benefits based on a third person's work record is deemed entitled on the worker beneficiary's record. Therefore, the worker beneficiary's earnings above the exempt amount would be charged not only against his or her own benefits and the benefits of those entitled on his or her record, but also against the spouse's or child's benefits that are based on a third person's work record. As noted previously, disabled beneficiaries are subject to different rules and limitations regarding earnings.

POLICY ISSUES

Policymakers have asked questions about the RET 's impact on labor supply and on the timing of Social Security benefit claims. Some argue that the RET is perceived as a "tax" on work effort, and that it induces workers to work fewer hours, or even to retire completely from the workforce. Another line of enquiry is whether the RET causes workers to delay claiming Social Security benefits. Both of these effects could have important implications for the retirement security of workers, their spouses and their survivors.

Quantitative studies have found mixed evidence concerning the RET's impact on work hours, retirement and the timing of Social Security benefit claims. Although the RET has been found to have a substantial effect on the labor supply of workers at or just above the annual RET threshold, the impact on workers with higher wages and salaries is more ambiguous. There is somewhat stronger evidence that the RET causes workers to delay claiming Social Security benefits.

The RET and Work Incentives

The impact of the RET on work hours varies by income level. At wages and salaries that are at or just above the annual RET threshold, the RET may encourage workers to work fewer hours, to keep wages or salaries just under the RET threshold. This effect is known as "bunching" or "clustering" under the RET threshold. A 1999 study found that a subset of workers do cluster at earnings levels just below the RET threshold.[20]

At higher earnings levels, the RET's impact on work hours is more ambiguous. Some workers perceive the RET as a tax on work effort (despite the recomputation of benefits at FRA). Moreover, other workers who are aware of the recomputation may place a relatively low value on future income. To the extent that the RET is perceived as a tax on earnings, it may induce some workers to reduce their work hours or even to retire completely from the workforce. Other workers, however, may respond to the RET reduction to Social Security benefits by working more, not fewer, hours to reach their income goals or requirements. For these workers, eliminating the RET would increase total income (income from labor plus income from Social Security). This has led some to argue that eliminating the RET would benefit some higher earners because the additional Social Security benefits that would become available would permit higher earners, if they wished, to reduce their work hours.

One study of the period from 1973 to 1998 found that the RET had little or no effect on the aggregate work hours and earnings of men aged 62 and older, although there is somewhat stronger evidence that the RET had an impact on women's earnings (no evidence was found for an impact on women's work hours).[21] However, a study of Social Security beneficiaries' response to the 2000 removal of the RET for beneficiaries at or above FRA found that, when workers are segmented by earnings level, fairly large effects on earnings are found, with the effects on earnings concentrated just below and above the RET threshold. (The study did not examine how work hours were affected by the 2000 change in the RET.)[22] Research has not found the RET to have a large effect on labor force participation, that is, a worker's decision to retire or remain in the workforce. This is perhaps in part because the RET is a relatively small part of the larger retirement decision that includes other factors such as pension rules and the worker's health, and also because it is difficult to separate the RET 's impact from the trend toward later retirement that is already under way.

The RET and Incentives to Claim Social Security Benefits

Because the RET applies to persons who are younger than FRA, it may discourage persons below the FRA from claiming benefits. As noted earlier, some workers perceive the RET as a "tax" on benefits received before FRA, even though the recomputation of benefits at FRA (which results in a higher monthly benefit starting at FRA) allows the worker to recoup benefits withheld under the RET.

The quantitative evidence that the RET has an impact on the decision concerning when to claim Social Security benefits is somewhat stronger than the quantitative evidence for the RET's impact on work and earnings. For example, the Gruber and Orszag study that examined persons aged 62 and older during the period from 1973 to 1998 estimated that a $1,000 increase in the RET threshold could increase the share of men aged 62 and older who receive Social Security benefits by 0.7% to 1.6%, while eliminating the RET could increase that share by 5.2% to 13.5%.[23] A more recent study that examined the 2000 elimination of the RET for men and women at or above FRA found a 2 to 5 percentage point increase in benefit claims among men and women aged 65 to 69, and a 3 to 5 percentage point increase among men and women who reach the age of 65.[24]

The RET, Retirement Security and Early Benefit Claims

Some argue that, to the extent the RET causes some workers to delay claiming Social Security benefits, this can be beneficial for the worker as well as for his or her spouse or survivor. Claiming Social Security benefits before the FRA can reduce a worker's Social Security benefit amount in two ways, as noted earlier: (1) through the RET, although when the worker attains FRA his or her benefits are recomputed and a higher monthly benefit amount is payable starting at FRA; and (2) through the actuarial reduction for early retirement which, although it is intended to be actuarially fair to the individual over his or her expected lifetime, causes a permanent reduction to the worker's monthly Social Security benefit amount.

As discussed, the RET applies to spousal benefits. (See section "The RET May Affect Social Security Benefits Received by Spouses, Survivors and Other Dependents.") Spousal benefits that have been reduced by the RET are restored starting when the spouse attains FRA. Spousal benefits are not restored, however, when the RET is applied to the benefits of a spouse who is already at or above FRA .(See "Benefits Withheld Under the RET are Restored Starting at FRA.")

Survivors' benefits may be permanently affected by the worker beneficiary's decision to claim benefits before FRA. Under a provision in the Social Security Act called the *widow(er)'s limit provision*, the widow(er)'s benefit may be reduced if the widow(er)'s benefit payable on the worker's record exceeds the benefit the worker was receiving (including any actuarial reduction for early retirement that may have reduced the worker's benefit) before his or her death.[25] If a worker has benefits withheld under the RET and he or she dies before attaining FRA (when the worker's benefit would have been recomputed), for purposes of determining the limit on the widow(er) 's benefit, the worker's benefit is recomputed at the time of the worker's death to take into account months for which no benefit or a partial benefit was paid as a result of the RET.

Elderly widows, in particular, may face reduced living standards if their spouses claim benefits before FRA, because of the actuarial reduction to benefits described above. Women tend to outlive their husbands and are therefore more likely than men to receive Social Security survivors' benefits. In addition, individuals and couples are more likely to deplete other assets later in retirement, leaving the couple or surviving spouse more reliant on Social Security.

Other Policy Issues

Some argue that eliminating the RET would have positive budgetary and economic effects because people would work more and pay more Social Security payroll and other taxes. The effect of the RET on labor supply is probably modest, however, as discussed above.

A common complaint among beneficiaries affected by the RET is that they are being denied a benefit they have "bought and paid for." A related argument is that the RET resembles a form of needs testing, making benefit receipt contingent on demonstrating "need" for this earned benefit. Supporters of the RET counter that Social Security is intended as a form of insurance against the risks of retirement and disability; just as the program does not pay disability benefits to those who are not disabled, it should not pay retirement benefits to those who are not retired.

The recomputation of benefits at FRA to restore benefits withheld under the RET is not widely known or understood. As noted previously, if a beneficiary has benefits withheld under the RET, his or her benefit is recomputed when he or she attains FRA to take into account months for which no benefit or a partial benefit was paid due to the RET. The recomputation results in a higher monthly benefit amount starting at FRA and allows the worker to recoup the value of any benefits "lost" under the RET, assuming he or she lives to average life expectancy. As a result, some observers argue that the RET should not be perceived as a "tax."[26] However, for some workers with shorter lifespans, the recovery of benefits may be incomplete. Conversely, for those who live longer than average, the recomputation may result in higher lifetime benefits that more than make up for the initial benefit reductions under the RET. Because life expectancy is linked to income, some argue that the RET may be regressive on a lifetime basis.[27]

Critics of the RET argue that it discriminates against claimants who must continue working to supplement their benefits. In contrast, claimants with no earnings who have other forms of income, such as private pensions or investment income, can receive full Social Security benefits. Supporters of the RET counter that eliminating the RET would provide a bonus to people who are fortunate enough to be able to continue working after becoming entitled to retirement benefits, and the additional Social Security benefits may allow or encourage some individuals to reduce their work hours.

Financial Effect of Repealing the RET on the Social Security Trust Fund

Under current law, the RET has no major effect on Social Security financing over the long run because, *on average*, the RET has "no significant effect" on lifetime benefits.[28] Therefore, the Social Security Administration's Office of the Chief Actuary (OCACT) estimates that elimination of the RET for individuals aged 62 or older would have no major effect on Social Security's projected long-range financial outlook.[29]

In the short run, however, OCACT estimates that elimination of the RET would have a negative effect on the Social Security trust fund in the amount of $81 billion from 2012 to 2018. The trust fund would experience a projected cash-flow deficit of $12.1 billion in 2012, and a projected cash-flow deficit of $10.4 billion in 2018. OCACT notes: "In the first several years after elimination of the retirement earnings test, benefit payments are projected to increase substantially, because benefits are paid under the proposal where such payments would be withheld, or the individual would have not applied for benefits yet, under current law."[30]

In summary, OCACT notes that the projected financial effects for the Social Security program of eliminating the RET are due to "(1) some individuals no longer having their benefits withheld, (2) some individuals who would apply for Social Security benefits earlier because of the earnings test elimination, and (3) a small net increase in earnings for individuals currently subject to the earnings test."[31]

Appendix A. Computation of the Social Security Retired-Worker Benefit

To be eligible for a Social Security retired-worker benefit, a person generally needs 40 earnings credits, or 10 years of Social Security-covered employment (among other requirements). A worker's initial monthly benefit is based on his or her 35 highest years of earnings which are indexed to historical wage growth (earnings through the age of 60 are indexed; earnings thereafter are counted at nominal value). The 35 highest years of indexed earnings are divided by 35 to determine the worker's career-average annual earnings. The resulting amount is divided by 12 to determine the worker's average indexed monthly earnings (AIME). If a worker has fewer than 35 years of earnings in covered employment, years of no earnings are entered as zeros.

The worker's basic benefit amount (i.e., before any adjustments for early or delayed retirement) is the primary insurance amount (PIA). The PIA is determined by applying a formula to the AIME as shown in **Table A-1**. First, the AIME is sectioned into three brackets, or levels, of earnings. Three progressive factors—90%, 32%, and 1 5%—are applied to the three different brackets of AIME. The three products derived from multiplying each factor and bracket of AIME are added together. For workers who become eligible for retirement benefits (i.e., those who attain age 62), become disabled, or die in 2010, the PIA is determined as shown in the example in Table A-1.

Table A- 1. Computation of a Worker's Primary Insurance Amount in 2010 Based on an Illustrative AIME of $5,000

Factors	Three Brackets of AIME (2010)	PIA for Worker with an Illustrative AIME of $5,000
90%	first $761 of AIME, plus	$684.90
32%	AIME over $761 and through $4,586, plus	$1,224.00
15%	AIME over $4,586	$62.10
Total (Worker's PIA)		**$1,971.00**

Source: Congressional Research Service.

Adjustment to Benefits Claimed before or after FRA

A worker's initial monthly benefit is equal to his or her PIA if he or she begins receiving benefits at FRA (i.e., FRA is the earliest age at which full (unreduced) retirement benefits are payable). A worker's initial monthly benefit will be *less* than his or her PIA if he or she begins receiving benefits *before* FRA, and it will be *greater* than his or her PIA if he or she begins receiving benefits *after* FRA. As noted previously, FRA ranges from the age of 65 to 67 depending on the person's year of birth.

Retirement benefits are reduced by five-ninths of 1% (or 0.0056) of the worker's PIA for each month of entitlement before FRA up to 36 months, for a reduction of about 6.7% a year. For each month of benefit entitlement before FRA in excess of 36 months, retirement benefits are reduced by five-twelfths of 1% (or 0.0042), for a reduction of 5% a year. Workers who delay filing for benefits until after FRA receive a delayed retirement credit (DRC). The DRC applies beginning with the month the worker attains FRA and ending with the month before he or she attains the age of 70. Starting in 1990, the DRC increased until it reached 8% per year for workers born in 1943 or later (i.e., starting with those who attained age 62 in 2005 or age 66 in 2009).[32]

APPENDIX B. SOCIAL SECURITY AUXILIARY BENEFITS (BENEFITS FOR THE WORKER'S FAMILY MEMBERS)

Social Security provides benefits to eligible family members of a retired, disabled or deceased worker. Benefits payable to family members are equal to a specified percentage of the worker's PIA, subject to a maximum family benefit amount.

Social Security provides a monthly benefit to the spouse or divorced spouse (if the marriage lasted 10 or more years) of an entitled retired or disabled worker equal to 50% of the worker's PIA.[33] A monthly survivor benefit equal to 100% of the deceased worker's PIA is payable to the surviving spouse or surviving divorced spouse of a worker who was fully insured at the time of death.[34] Benefits for spouses, divorced spouses and surviving spouses are reduced if claimed before FRA. In addition, these benefits are reduced or fully offset if the beneficiary receives his or her own Social Security retired-worker benefit or a pension from a job that was not covered by Social Security (such as certain federal, state or local government jobs).

The child of a disabled or retired worker is eligible for 50% of the worker's PIA. The child of a deceased worker is eligible for 75% of the worker's PIA.[35] Social Security also provides a monthly mother's or father's benefit, equal to 75% of the worker's PIA, to a surviving parent of any age who cares for the deceased worker's child, when that child is under the age of 16 or disabled.

Table B-1. Social Security Auxiliary Benefits

Basis for Entitlement	Basic Eligibility Requirements	Basic Benefit Amount Before Any Adjustments
Spouse	At least age 62	50% of worker's PIA
	The worker on whose record benefits are based must be receiving benefits.	
Divorced Spouse	At least age 62	50% of worker's PIA
(if divorced individual was married to the worker for at least 10 years before the divorce became final and is currently unmarried)	Generally, the worker on whose record benefits are based must be receiving benefits. However, a divorced spouse may receive benefits on the	

Table B-1. (Continued)

Basis for Entitlement	Basic Eligibility Requirements	Basic Benefit Amount Before Any Adjustments
	worker's record if the worker is eligible for (but not receiving) benefits and the divorce has been final for at least two years.	
Widow(er) & Divorced Widow(er)	At least age 60	100% of worker's PIA
(if divorced individual was married to the worker for at least 10 years before the divorce became final and did not remarry before age 60)		
Disabled Widow(er) & Divorced Disabled Widow(er)	At least age 50 The qualifying disability must have occurred:	100% of worker's PIA
(if divorced individual was married to the worker for at least 10 years before the divorce became final and did not remarry before age 50)	(1) before or within seven years of the worker's death; or (2) within seven years of having been previously entitled to benefits on the worker's record as a widow(er) with a child in his or her care; or (3) within seven years of having been previously entitled to benefits as a disabled widow(er) that ended because the qualifying disability ended (whichever is later).	
Mothers and Fathers	Surviving parent of any age who cares for the deceased worker's child, when that child is either under the age of 16 or disabled. Eligibility generally ceases if the surviving mother or father remarries.	75% of deceased worker's PIA (subject to the maximum family benefit amount)

Table B-1. (Continued)

Basis for Entitlement	Basic Eligibility Requirements	Basic Benefit Amount Before Any Adjustments
Parents	At least age 62 and has not married since the worker's death. The parent must have been receiving at least one-half of his or her support from the worker at the time of the worker's death or, if the worker had a period of disability which continued until death, at the beginning of the period of disability.	If one parent is entitled to benefits: 82.5% of deceased worker's PIA If two parents are entitled to benefits: 75% of deceased worker's PIA (for each) (subject to the maximum family benefit amount)
Child	A child (including a dependent, unmarried biological child, adopted child, stepchild, and, in some cases, grandchild) of a retired, disabled, or deceased worker who was fully or currently insured at the time of death. The child must be: (1) under age 18; or (2) a full-time elementary or secondary student under age 19; or (3) a disabled person aged 18 or older whose disability began before age 22.	50% of worker's PIA for child of a retired or disabled worker 75% of deceased worker's PIA for child of a deceased worker (subject to the maximum family benefit amount)

Source: Congressional Research Service.

Notes: The maximum family benefit may apply, reducing the benefit received by each family member on a proportional basis. The maximum family benefit varies from 150% to 188% of a retired or deceased worker's PIA. For the family of a worker who is entitled to disability benefits, the maximum family benefit is the lesser of 85% of the worker's AIME or 150% of the worker's PIA, but no less than 100% of the worker's PIA.

Table B-1 provides a summary of Social Security auxiliary benefits for the family of a retired, disabled or deceased worker, including eligibility requirements related to age and other factors.

Maximum Family Benefit Amount

The total amount of benefits payable to a family based on a retired or deceased worker's record is capped by the maximum family benefit amount. The maximum family benefit varies from 150% to 188% of the retired or deceased worker's PIA, and the maximum family benefit cannot be exceeded regardless of the number of beneficiaries entitled to benefits on the worker's record. If the sum of all benefits based on the worker's record exceeds the maximum family benefit amount, each dependent's or survivor's benefit is reduced in equal proportion to bring the total amount of benefits within the family maximum. For the family of a worker who attains age 62 in 2010, or dies in 2010 before attaining age 62, the total amount of benefits payable is limited to

- 150% of the first $972 of PIA, plus
- 272% of PIA over $972 and through $1,403, plus
- 134% of PIA over $1,403 and through $1,830, plus
- 175% of PIA over $1,830.

The dollar amounts in the maximum family benefit formula are indexed to average wage growth, as in the primary benefit formula. A separate maximum family benefit formula applies to the family of a worker who is entitled to disability benefits.

Appendix C. Annual Exempt Amounts under the Social Security Retirement Earnings Test, Calendar Years 2000-2010

The RET annual exempt amount is indexed to average wage growth in the economy. An exception, however, is that the annual exempt amount is not increased in a year during which no Social Security cost-of-living adjustment (COLA) is payable. In 2010, there was no Social Security COLA, therefore the RET exempt amount did not increase.

The RET applies only to wage and salary income (i.e., earnings from work). It does not apply to "unearned" income, such as income from pensions, rents, dividends, or interest.

Table C- 1. Annual Exempt Amounts Under the Social Security Retirement Earnings Test, Calendar Years 2000-2010

Calendar Year	Prior to Year of Attaining FRA	During Year of Attaining FRA
2000	$10,080	$17,000
2001	$10,680	$25,000
2002	$11,280	$30,000
2003	$11,520	$30,720
2004	$11,640	$31,080
2005	$12,000	$31,800
2006	$12,480	$33,240
2007	$12,960	$34,440
2008	$13,560	$36,120
2009	$14,160	$37,680
2010	$14,160	$37,680

Source: Social Security Administration, *http://www.socialsecurity.gov/ OACT /COLA/ rtea.html.*

End Notes

[1] The Social Security FRA is increasing gradually from age 65 to age 67 for workers born in 1938 or later; it will reach age 67 for workers born in 1960 or later. The FRA is 66 for workers who attain age 62 in 2010 (workers born in 1948) and workers who attain age 65 in 2010 (workers born in 1945). A person who claims benefits at FRA will receive full (unreduced) benefits. Workers may claim retirement benefits as early as age 62, however, a worker who claims benefits before FRA is subject to an actuarial reduction to benefits for early retirement that is unrelated to the RET.

[2] The Social Security Administration defines "excess earnings," for people who are below FRA and will not attain FRA during the calendar year, as 50% of earnings above the annual exempt amount. For people who will attain FRA during the calendar year, "excess earnings" are defined as 33 1/3% of earnings above the annual exempt amount (20 C.F.R. § 404.430(b)). This definition is helpful for understanding the method of charging excess earnings against monthly benefits as described in the regulations (20 C.F.R. § 404.434(b)).

[3] Committee on Economic Security, *Report of the Committee on Economic Security*, Washington, DC, January 1935, http://www.socialsecurity.gov/history/reports/ces5.html, in the section entitled "Contributory Annuities (Compulsory System): Outline of Plan."

[4] P.L. 74-271, the Social Security Act of 1935, Sec. 202(d), *http://www.ssa.gov/ history/ 35actii.html#Old-Benefit.*

[5] P.L. 76-379, the Social Security Act Amendments of 1939, Sec. 203(d)(1) and Sec. 203(e), http://www.socialsecurity.gov/history/pdf/1939Act.pdf.

[6] For workers who claim benefits before FRA, the monthly benefit amount is decreased by an adjustment that is roughly actuarially fair. The purpose of the actuarial reduction is to ensure that the worker receives roughly the same total lifetime benefits regardless of when he or she claims benefits between age 62 and FRA (assuming he or she lives to average life expectancy). Benefits taken before FRA are reduced about 6.7% per year for the first three

years of benefit entitlement before FRA (i.e., the first 36 months from age 62 to age 65) and 5% per year thereafter. For example, for a worker whose FRA is 66, claiming benefits at age 62 results in an initial monthly benefit that is 25% lower than his or her PIA ((6.7% * 3 years) + (5% * 1 year)). Workers who delay filing for benefits until after FRA receive a delayed retirement credit (DRC). The DRC applies beginning with the month the worker attains FRA and ending with the month before he or she attains age 70. Starting in 1990, the DRC increased until it reached 8% per year for workers born in 1943 or later (i.e., starting with those who attained age 62 in 2005 or age 66 in 2009).

[7] Beneficiaries of Social Security Disability Insurance (SSDI) are subject to different rules and limitations regarding earnings. The limitations on earnings for SSDI beneficiaries are referred to as substantial gainful activity (SGA) amounts. The SGA differs from the RET in that a disability beneficiary whose earnings exceed the SGA threshold, after a trial work period, will lose eligibility for Social Security disability benefits. By contrast, a person whose earnings exceed the annual RET threshold may receive partial or full Social Security benefits for any months of the year after the RET charge has been applied. In addition, the benefit recomputation at FRA results in an upward adjustment of the Social Security benefit amount to reflect any months in which benefits were withheld in full or in part under the RET. In 2010, the SGA amount for non-blind beneficiaries is $1,000 a month (net of impairment-related work expenses). For blind beneficiaries, the SGA amount is $1,640 a month. Both amounts generally increase with the increase in average wages. For purposes of SSDI, a "disability" is defined as the inability to engage in substantial gainful activity by reason of a medically determinable physical or mental impairment expected to result in death or last at least 12 months. For more information, see CRS Report RL32279, *Primer on Disability Benefits: Social Security Disability Insurance (SSDI) and Supplemental Security Income (SSI)*, by Scott Szymendera.

[8] Beneficiaries who will attain FRA during the calendar year are treated differently as a result of a compromise reached when the RET structure was modified in 2000. Before 2000, there were two RETs, one for beneficiaries below FRA and one for beneficiaries between FRA and age 70. The RET for beneficiaries between FRA and age 70 was more generous; the exempt amount was higher and the reduction to benefits was $1 for each $3 of earnings above that amount. By comparison, the RET for beneficiaries below FRA applied a lower exempt amount and the reduction to benefits was $1 for each $2 of earnings above that amount. In 2000, when Congress eliminated the RET for beneficiaries beginning with the month they attain FRA, there was a concern that beneficiaries who would attain FRA in 2000 would be worse off. The concern arose because, under pre-2000 law, the more generous RET applied to beneficiaries starting in January of the year they attained FRA. Therefore, eliminating the more generous RET would cause these beneficiaries to be subject to the lower exempt amount and the 50% offset during that year. To address this concern, the House version of the legislation, for 2000 only, allowed beneficiaries attaining FRA in 2000 to be subject to the more generous RET in the months preceding attainment of FRA. A Senate Manager's Amendment extended this provision to all future beneficiaries for the year they attain FRA. In April 2000, President Clinton signed the legislation, which became P.L. 106-182.

[9] The annual exempt amounts are not increased in a year during which no Social Security cost-of-living adjustment is payable.

[10] The dually entitled beneficiary's earnings above the exempt amount will not affect the retired-worker benefit received by the worker on whose record the spousal benefit is based.

[11] In addition, if a beneficiary continues to work, the Social Security Administration automatically checks the person's record each year to determine if the additional earnings will increase his or her monthly benefit. For example, earnings for 2010 would be included in a recomputation effective January 2011. See Social Security Administration, *Program Operations Manual System* (Washington, DC), RS 00605.401, *http://policy.ssa.gov/poms.nsf/links/0300605401.*

[12] Under current law, the maximum reduction for early retirement ranges from 20% for a worker whose FRA is 65 to 30% for a worker whose FRA is 67.

[13] To simplify the example, it is assumed that the person was born on January 1. Therefore, there is no need to take into account the different annual exempt amount and benefit reduction rate that apply during the calendar year in which a beneficiary attains FRA. It is also assumed that the person both works and collects benefits over each full calendar year, so the "grace year" provision does not apply.

[14] For example, a person who has earnings of $26,160 in 2010 and a monthly Social Security benefit of $1,000 (or $12,000 in annual benefits) would be subject to a 50% reduction in Social Security benefits in 2010 under the RET. The person's benefits would be fully withheld for the first six months of 2010.

[15] A family's total benefits are subject to a cap known as the "family maximum," as discussed in Appendix B. For purposes of illustration, this example is simplified and does not include the family maximum.

[16] Social Security Administration, *Program Operations Manual System* (Washington, DC), RS 02501.110, http://policy.ssa.gov/poms.nsf/links/0302501110.

[17] An example of such a couple would be a worker beneficiary who receives a retired-worker benefit based on his or her own work record and an auxiliary beneficiary (a spouse) who is currently working but does not receive his or her own retired-worker benefit. This may be the case, for example, because the auxiliary beneficiary (the spouse) does not have enough Social Security-covered employment to qualify for a retirement benefit.

[18] 20 C.F.R. § 404.434(b)(3).

[19] If the auxiliary beneficiary in this example (spouse #2) were dually entitled to a retired-worker benefit based on his or her own work record and a spousal benefit, the worker beneficiary's RET charge would apply only to the spousal benefit, and not the retired-worker benefit, received by spouse #2.

[20] Leora Friedberg, *The Labor Supply Effects of the Social Security Earnings Test*, National Bureau of Economic Research, Working Paper No. 7200, Cambridge, MA, June 1999, http://www.nber.org/papers/w7200.

[21] Jonathan Gruber and Peter Orszag, *Does the Social Security Earnings Test Affect Labor Supply and Benefits Receipt?*, National Bureau of Economic Research, Working Paper No. 7923, Cambridge, MA, September 2000, http://www.nber.org/papers/w7923.

[22] Jae G. Song and Joyce Manchester, "How Have People Responded to Changes in the Retirement Earnings Test in 2000," *Social Security Bulletin*, vol. 67, no. 1 (2007), http://www.ssa.gov/policy/docs/ssb/v67n1/v67n1p1.pdf.

[23] Jonathan Gruber and Peter Orszag, *Does the Social Security Earnings Test Affect Labor Supply and Benefits Receipt?*, National Bureau of Economic Research, Working Paper No. 7923, Cambridge, MA, September 2000, http://www.nber.org/papers/w7923.

[24] Jae G. Song and Joyce Manchester, "How Have People Responded to Changes in the Retirement Earnings Test in 2000," *Social Security Bulletin*, vol. 67, no. 1 (2007), http://www.ssa.gov/policy/docs/ssb/v67n1/v67n1p1.pdf.

[25] Under the *widow(er) 's limit provision,* the widow(er)'s benefit is limited to the higher of: (1) the benefit the worker would be receiving if he or she were still alive and (2) 82.5% of the worker's PIA. For more information, see David A. Weaver, *The Widow(er)'s Limit Provision of Social Security,* Social Security Administration, Office of Policy, Research, Evaluation and Statistics, Working Paper Series Number 92, June 2001.

[26] Adam Paul, "The Tax That Wasn't," *The American: The Journal of the American Enterprise Institute*, December 17, 2009, http://blog.american.com/?p=8363.

[27] Jonathan Gruber and Peter Orszag, *What To Do About The Social Security Earnings Test?*, Center for Retirement Research, Boston, MA, July 1999, p. 5, http://crr.bc.edu/images/stories/Briefs/ib_1.pdf?phpMyAdmin= 43ac483c4de9t51d9eb41.

[28] Social Security Administration, Office of the Chief Actuary, *Estimated Long-Range OASDI Financial Effect of Repealing the Retirement Earnings Test at Ages 62 and Later*, April 30, 2010, p. 1 (hereinafter *SSA Cost Estimate for Repeal of the RET*).

[29] *SSA Cost Estimate for Repeal of the RET*. The estimate assumes that the RET would be eliminated starting in 2012 and is based on the intermediate assumptions of the 2009 Social Security Trustees Report. OCACT estimates that the policy change would reduce Social Security's projected long-range (average 75-year) funding shortfall from an amount equal to 2.00% of taxable payroll to an amount equal to 1.99% of taxable payroll.

[30] *SSA Cost Estimate for Repeal of the RET*, p. 2.

[31] *SSA Cost Estimate for Repeal of the RET*, p. 1.

[32] Other benefit adjustments may apply, such as those related to simultaneous entitlement to more than one type of Social Security benefit, receipt of a pension from work that was not covered by Social Security (a non-covered pension), the Social Security maximum family benefit, and the Social Security Retirement Earnings Test which is the focus of this chapter. For more information on the various benefit adjustments, see House Ways and Means Committee, 2008 Green Book, Section 1, Social Security: The Old-Age, Survivors, and Disability Insurance (OASDI) Programs, pp. 1-59 to 1-68, *http://waysandmeans.house.gov/media/pdf/111/ssgb.pdf*.

[33] The qualifying spouse must be at least age 62 or have a qualifying child (a child who is under age 16 or disabled) in his or her care. A spouse's benefit is reduced if he or she begins receiving benefits before FRA.

[34] The surviving spouse must be at least age 60 (or at least age 50 if disabled) and must not have remarried before age 60 (or age 50 if disabled).

[35] The child must be (1) under age 18; or (2) a full-time elementary or secondary student under age 19; or (3) a disabled person aged 18 or older whose disability began before age 22.

In: Social Security: Background, Issues and...
Editors: Jacob T. Álvarez
ISBN: 978-1-61761-469-9

Chapter 5

SOCIAL SECURITY: RAISING OR ELIMINATING THE TAXABLE EARNINGS BASE

Janemarie Mulvey

SUMMARY

Social Security taxes are levied on covered earnings up to a maximum level set each year. In 2010, this maximum—or what is referred to as the taxable earnings base—is $106,800. The taxable earnings base serves as both a cap on contributions and a cap on benefits. As a contribution base, it establishes the maximum amount of each worker's earnings that is subject to the payroll tax. As a benefit base, it establishes the maximum amount of earnings used to calculate benefits.

Since 1982, the Social Security taxable earnings base has risen at the same rate as average wages in the economy. However, because of increasing earnings inequality, the percentage of covered earnings that are taxable has decreased from 90% in 1982 to 85% in 2005. The percentage of covered earnings that is taxable is projected to decline to about 83% for 2014 and later. Because the cap was indexed to the average growth in wages, the share of the population below the cap has remained relatively stable at roughly 94%. Of the 9.5 million Americans with earnings above the base, roughly 80% are men and only 9% had any earnings from self-employment income. The District of

Columbia has the highest share of the population above the maximum (12%) and South Dakota has the lowest share (2%).

CRS estimated the potential impact of eliminating the taxable wage base on future benefits and taxes. If the base were removed in 2013, CRS estimates that by 2035, 21% of beneficiaries would have paid some additional payroll taxes over the course of their lifetimes. However, the average change in taxes and benefits would be small. Looking *only* at individuals who would pay any additional taxes over the course of their lifetimes, at the median, total lifetime tax payments would rise by 3% and benefits would increase by 2% relative to current law. In general, those in the highest income groups would have the largest changes in both tax payments and in benefits relative to current law.

Raising or eliminating the cap on wages that are subject to taxes could reduce the long-range deficit in the Social Security Trust Funds. For example, if the maximum taxable earnings amount had been raised in 2005 from $90,000 to $150,000—roughly the level needed to cover 90% of all earnings—it would have eliminated roughly 40% of the long-range shortfall in Social Security. If all earnings were subject to the payroll tax, but the base was retained for benefit calculations, the Social Security Trust Funds would remain solvent for the next 75 years. However, having different bases for contributions and benefits would weaken the traditional link between the taxes workers pay into the system and the benefits they receive.

BACKGROUND

Since the beginning of the program, Social Security taxes have been levied on covered earnings up to a maximum level set each year, referred to as the taxable earnings base. Social Security was enacted in 1935, and the Social Security payroll tax was first levied in 1937. From 1937 through 1949, the tax rate was 1% (on employee and employer, each) on earnings up to $3,000 a year. Since that time the rate has risen to 6.2% and the taxable earnings base has been increased to help meet the financing needs of the program, and to keep up to date with changing earnings levels. Since 1982, the Social Security earnings base has risen at the same rate as wages in the economy. By law, the Commissioner of Social Security is required to raise the base whenever an automatic benefit increase—cost of living adjustment (COLA)—is granted to Social Security recipients, assuming wages have risen. The increase in the base from 2009 to in 2010 is based on the increase in average wages from 2007 to 2008.[1]

Origin and History of the Taxable Earnings Base

In 1935, the designers of Social Security, President Franklin Roosevelt's Committee on Economic Security, did not recommend a maximum level of taxable earnings in its plan, and the draft bill that President Roosevelt sent to the Hill did not include one. The bill emphasized who was to be covered by the system, not how much wages should be taxed. Being in the midst of the Depression, the Administration's attention was on the large number of aged people living in poverty. Its goal in proposing a Social Security program was to complement public assistance measures (Old-Age Assistance) in its plan. The plan offered immediate cash aid to the aged poor and created an earnings-replacement system intended to lessen the need for welfare benefits in the long run. It was recognized that the new system would not be sufficient to provide full income in retirement, but would provide a "core" benefit as a floor of protection against poverty. Not concerned about high-income retirees, the Administration's proposal exempted non-manual workers earning $250 or more a month from coverage (i.e., $3,000 on an annual basis). Manual workers were to be covered regardless of their earnings, but few had earnings above this level.

It was the Social Security bill reported by the House Ways and Means Committee that clearly established a maximum taxable amount, which it set at $3,000 per year.[2] In addition, the committee dropped the exemption for non-manual workers with high earnings. The committee's report and floor statements made at the time give no clear record as to the reasoning for the taxable limit, but concerns about tax equity and attaining as much program coverage of the workforce as possible were suggested as factors for rejecting the high-earner exemption. Not covering them meant that they would not pay the tax where lower-wage earners would, and coverage would be erratic for workers whose earnings fluctuated above and below the $250 monthly threshold.

Although tax policy concerns were raised in later years, with a higher base preferred by those seeking a more proportional tax system, there was little if any serious attention given to eliminating the base entirely. In the late 1940s and early 1950s and to a lesser extent later on, the major arguments were over the base's size and how it affected the development of Social Security. A larger base meant that more earnings would be credited to a person's Social Security record and would lead to higher benefits (since benefits are based on a worker's earnings). Proponents argued that the base needed to be raised to reflect wage or price growth so that the benefits of moderate and well-to-do recipients would not erode over time (thereby preserving their support for the system). Critics argued that this would increase benefits for people who could save on their own while making saving by private means more difficult. In 1972, as a means of financing COLAs for Social Security recipients, procedures were enacted that increased the base automatically to reflect the growth in average wages. In 1977, the base was raised beyond what resulted from the automatic increase provision (by $7,500 over three years) as a means of raising revenue to help shore up the program's ailing financial condition. These ad hoc adjustments were intended to achieve a base under which 90% of all covered payroll would be subject to tax.

Medicare was enacted in 1965 with the hospital insurance (HI) portion of the program financed with payroll taxes. The HI tax was first levied in 1966 at a rate of 0.35% (on employee and employer, each) and the maximum taxable amount was set at the same level as Social Security's.[3] The HI rate was subsequently raised periodically (reaching its current level of 1.45% in 1986) to meet the financing needs of the program. However, its base continued to be the same as Social Security's through 1990. Then, to reduce federal budget deficits, the Omnibus Budget Reconciliation Act of 1990 (P.L. 101-518) raised the HI base to $125,000. The HI base then rose automatically to $135,000 over the next two years. In 1993, as part of his plan to reduce budget deficits, President Clinton proposed that the HI base be eliminated entirely. As part of the Omnibus Budget Reconciliation Act of 1993 (P.L. 103-66) the HI base was removed, raising an estimated $29 billion in revenues over the FY1994-FY1998 period. As there is no maximum taxable earnings amount in Medicare, Medicare financing will not be discussed further in this chapter.

The Taxable Earnings Base

The Taxable Earnings Base Today

In 2010, an estimated 162 million workers will pay Federal Insurance Contributions Act (FICA) taxes and Self-Employment Contributions Act (SECA) taxes on their wages and net self- employment income.[4] Both employers and employees contribute earnings at the FICA rate and SECA taxes are paid by the self-employed. Both taxes have three components: Old Age and Survivors Insurance (OASI), Disability Insurance (DI), and the HI part of Medicare. The OASDI tax is levied on earnings up to $106,800 in 2010. The HI tax is levied on all earnings.

The taxable earnings base limits the amount of wages or self-employment income used to calculate contributions to Social Security. Unlike income taxes, workers who have earnings over the limit, whether they earn $110,000 or $1 million, pay the same dollar amount in Social Security payroll taxes. Under the 2010 limit of $106,800, the maximum amount a wage and salary worker contributes to Social Security is $6,622 (his or her employer contribute an equal amount) whereas a self-employed individual contributes a maximum of $1 3,243.[5]

Table 1. 2010 Social Security and Medicare Tax Rates and Maximum Taxable Earnings, Maximum Taxes Paid, and Maximum Retirement Benefits

FICA and SECA Tax Rates:	**FICA**	**SECA**[a]
Old-Age and Survivors Insurance	5.30%	10.60%
+Disability Insurance	0.90%	1.80%
=Subtotal Social Security (OASDI) tax rate	*6.20%*	*12.40%*
+ Hospital Insurance tax rate	1.45%	2.90%
Total FICA and SECA Rate	**7.65%**	**15.30%**
Combined Employee and Employer FICA Tax Rates:		
Employee	7.65%	
+Employer	7.65%	
Combined FICA Rate	**15.30%**	
Maximum Taxable Earnings:		
Social Security	$106,800	
Hospital Insurance	no maximum	
Maximum FICA/SECA Taxes:	**OASDI**	**HI**
Employee/Employer (each):	$6,622	No limit
Self-Employed:	$13,243	No limit
Social Security Benefit for 2010 Retiree With Earnings at or Above the Maximum for Entire Career		
	Monthly	**Annual**
Retired at age 62:	$1,824	$21,888
Retired at full retirement age (66):	$2,346	$28,152

Source: SSA http://www.ssa.gov/pressoffice/factsheets/colafacts2010.pdf.
Certain adjustments and income tax deductions apply.

The taxable earnings base also limits the annual amount of earnings that are used in benefit calculations and thus sets a ceiling on the amount Social Security pays in benefits. For example, the maximum amount of earnings in 2010 used to calculate a worker's benefit is $106,800, regardless of whether the worker earned above that amount. If an individual earned at or above the earnings base for his or her entire career[6] and retired in 2010 at the full retirement age, his or her annual benefit would be $28,164 ($2,347 per month), the maximum benefit payable under current law.[7] However, very few Americans receive the maximum benefit as it is extremely rare to have had such consistently high earnings over a lifetime.

The Taxable Earnings Base over Time

The portion of Social Security covered earnings that are subject to the payroll tax has fluctuated over time (**Figure 1**).

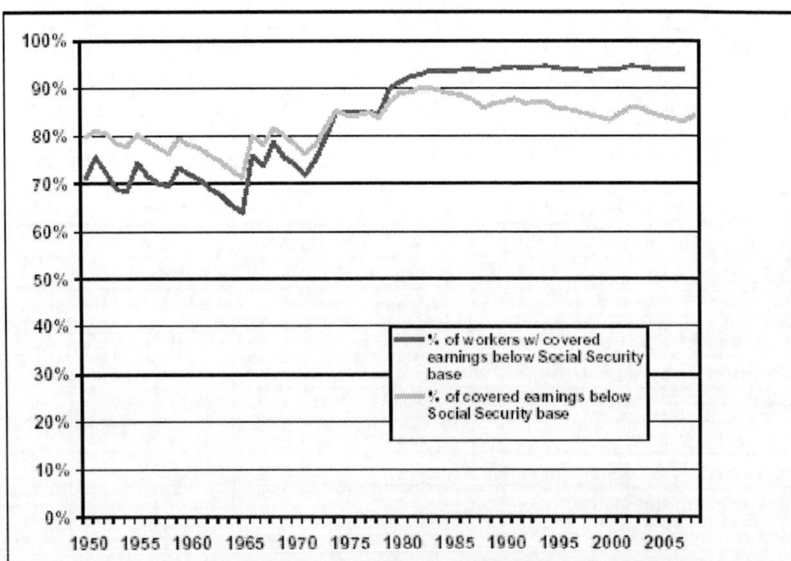

Source: Figure prepared by the Congressional Research Service (CRS), based on data from the Social Security Administration, Annual Supplement, 2009.

Figure 1. Share of Earnings and Workers Below the Taxable Earnings Base, 1950-2007

When the program began in 1937, taxable earnings represented 92% of covered earnings (Table A-1). By 1965, this ratio had dropped to its low of 71%. Prior to 1972, the taxable earnings base was updated periodically by Congress, which contributed to its dramatic fluctuations in the 1950s and 1960s. Since 1972, the base has been indexed to the increase in wages in the economy, which has reduced the volatility somewhat. As described earlier, to raise revenue, Congress raised the taxable earnings base in the 1977 amendments to the Social Security Act to a level that would cover 90% of aggregate earnings by 1982.

Since the 1980s, the share of covered *workers* below the taxable earnings base has remained relatively stable at roughly 94%. However, the share of covered *earnings* that are taxed has fallen from 90% of all earnings in 1982 to 83% in 2007. The large declines in the late 1990s were mainly because salaries for top earners grew faster than the pay of workers below the cap.[8]

The Taxable Earnings Base by State

In 2007, 6% of workers had earnings above the taxable base of $90,000.[9] However, focusing on the nationwide average hides the diversity among the states and the District of Columbia. The share of the population above the base ranges from a high in the District of Columbia, where 12% of covered workers earn above the base, to a low in South Dakota, where 2% of workers earn above this amount (Table A-2). The states with the lowest share of workers over the base are South Dakota, Mississippi, Arkansas, North Dakota, and Montana. Those with the highest share of workers over the base are the District of Columbia, New Jersey, Connecticut, Massachusetts, and Maryland.

The Taxable Earnings Base by Employment Status and Gender

According to statistics from the Social Security Administration, a small share of workers earn above the taxable earnings base each year. In 2007, 6% of workers (10.0 million individuals) earned more than the taxable earnings base (Table A-3).[10] Most of the individuals earning above the base were men (7.4 million individuals or roughly 80% of the total). In 2007, 9% of all male workers and 3% of all female workers had earnings above the maximum. Most individuals earning above the base were wage and salary workers (roughly

93% of the total). Only 6.4% of individuals who earned above the base were self-employed.

The Future of the Taxable Earnings Base

The taxable wage base is increased annually by the average growth in wages, so the share of the population below the cap is expected to remain relatively stable over time. However, because of increasing earnings inequality, the share of payroll that is taxed is expected to decline even further. Under the intermediate assumptions of the 2007 Trustees Report, the percentage of covered earnings that is taxable is projected to decline to about 83% for 2015. However, the Trustees Report assumes the levels will remain stable thereafter.

Projections of the Share of the Population Earning above the Taxable Wage Base over Their Lifetime

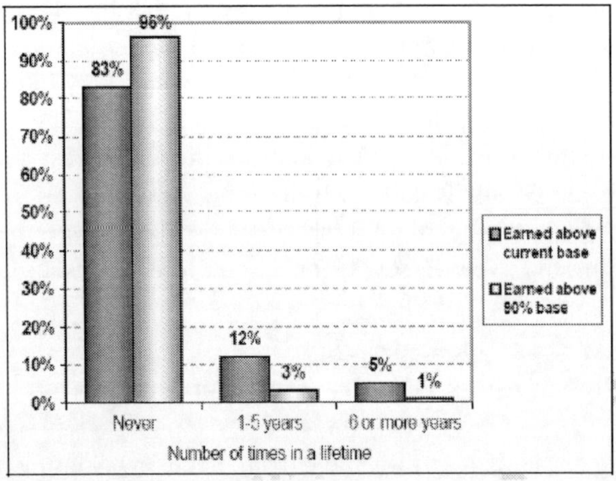

Source: CRS calculations using the Urban Institute's Dynasim microsimulation model.

Figure 2. Share of the Population with Earnings Above the Taxable Wage Base Over Their Lifetime

Workers' earnings rise and fall during their careers, so any analysis of the population that earns above the taxable wage base in a given year is limited in that it may miss individuals who were above the base in previous years or will have earnings above the base in the future. To address this issue, CRS used the Dynasim microsimulation model to estimate the share of individuals in the future who will *ever* have earned above the current-law taxable wage base over the course of their lifetimes.[11]

In 2007, 6% of workers earned more than the taxable earnings base.[12] The Dynasim model projects this share will remain relatively constant over time. Although a small share of workers are projected to earn above the taxable earnings base in a given year, the model estimates that roughly one in five individuals would earn above the maximum at some point in their lifetimes (Figure 2). The model projects that 12% of workers would earn above the earnings base for between one and five years over the course of their working lives. Few individuals sustain the high earnings for long periods in their careers. The model estimates that only 5% of workers would earn above the taxable wage base for more than five years.[13]

Few individuals have earnings higher than a level of taxable earnings that would cover 90% of aggregate earnings (the level Congress attempted to achieve when it last addressed Social Security's finances). The Dynasim model projects that roughly 1% of workers have earnings above a 90% limit each year. In other words, due to high levels of earnings inequality, roughly 1% of the population earn 10% of all the earnings.[14] Looking over the course of an individual's lifetime, the model projects that less than 4% of the population would ever earn above the 90% base and nearly all of those who do would earn above the base for less than five years (Figure 2).

Impact of Raising or Eliminating the Taxable Earnings Base

Raising or removing the taxable earnings base could reduce or eliminate the long-term Social Security deficit. [15] The additional tax revenues would be substantial. However, the full impact of the policy change would depend on whether the wages above the maximum would also be counted toward benefits. Raising or eliminating the taxable earnings base while maintaining the current benefit structure, where benefits are calculated on the full contribution base, would lead to higher monthly Social Security checks for individuals who earned more than the taxable wage base during their careers. These higher benefit payments would lead to greater program outlays, although these expenditures would be more than offset by greater tax revenues. While the solvency impact would be improved to a greater degree if the cap on taxes was eliminated and the cap on benefits was retained, the traditional link between contributions and benefits would be broken.

Rather than eliminate the taxable wage base, policymakers could set it to cover a constant share of aggregate earnings. As described previously, the portion of Social Security covered earnings subject to the payroll tax has fluctuated since its inception. Rising inequality—primarily increases in the earnings of the highest paid individuals—has led to a decline in the share of U.S. earnings that is taxed. The proportion of earnings that is taxed is projected to continue to fall. Maintaining a consistent tax base would increase revenue and help to improve the system's solvency. Some have proposed raising the taxable earnings base to consistently tax 90% of aggregate U.S. earnings—restoring it to roughly the level in 1982 when Congress last addressed Social Security's finances. The Social Security Administration and the Joint Committee on Tax have also used this benchmark to analyze the impact of raising the base on the Social Security trust funds and the budget.

The following sections examine the impact of raising or eliminating the taxable wage base on individuals, the Social Security trust funds, on federal revenue, and on workers' and employers' behavior.

Impact on Individuals' Lifetime Payroll Taxes and Social Security Benefits if the Taxable Wage Base Were Eliminated

To estimate how much individuals' taxes and benefits would rise if the wage base were eliminated, CRS has used the Dynasim microsimulation model to look at Social Security beneficiaries in the year 2035. The estimates assume the taxable wage base would be completely eliminated starting in 2013 for calculating both the payroll taxes and future Social Security benefits. The following sections detail the impact of eliminating the base on beneficiaries based on their income and gender.[16]

Aggregate Changes

If the base were removed, the majority of beneficiaries would pay no additional taxes compared with current law, as fewer than 8% of workers are projected to earn above the taxable wage base each year. Examining the impact on individuals receiving Social Security benefits in 2035, roughly one in five beneficiaries (21%) would have paid any additional taxes over their lifetimes compared with current law (Figure 3). For most of these affected individuals, the increase would be moderate. Roughly 16% of all beneficiaries would see their lifetime tax payments increase by less than 10%. However, 3% of all beneficiaries would have their tax payments increase by 10% to 19%, and 2% would have tax increases of 20% or more.

To maintain the traditional link between contribution and benefits, policymakers could choose to calculate benefits based on a worker's total earnings, including those above the taxable wage base. Under this option, some beneficiaries would receive higher Social Security benefits. CRS estimates that 23% of beneficiaries in 2035 would have higher benefits than under current law. This share of beneficiaries who receive higher benefits is greater than the share of individuals who pay higher taxes because some low earners receive benefits based on their spouses' higher earnings. Most of the affected beneficiaries (20%) would see their benefits increase by less than 10% relative to current law. Only 3% of beneficiaries would see their benefits increase by 10% or more.

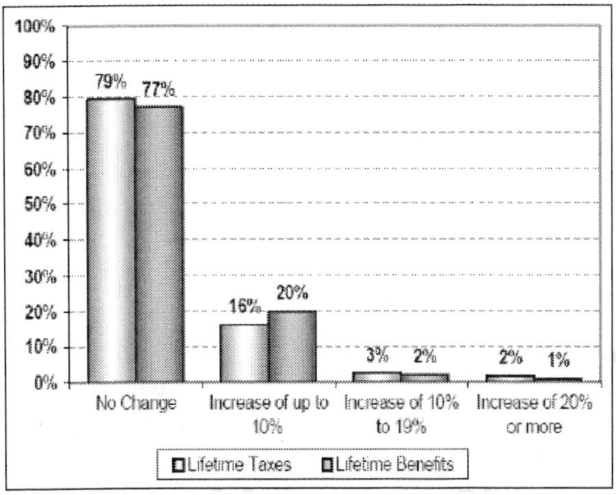

Source: CRS calculations using the Urban Institute's Dynasim microsimulation model.
Note: Lifetime taxes include both individual and employer OASDI contributions or self-employment contributions throughout the individual's entire career.

Figure 3. Share of Beneficiaries in 2035 with Tax and Benefit Increases Compared with Current Law If the Taxable Earnings Base Is Eliminated, by Level of Increase

Although 21% of beneficiaries in 2035 would pay some additional payroll taxes over the course of their lifetimes if the base were removed, the average change in taxes and benefits would be small. Looking *only* at individuals who would pay higher taxes over the course of their lifetimes, at the median, total lifetime tax payments would rise by 3% and benefits would increase by 2% relative to current law.

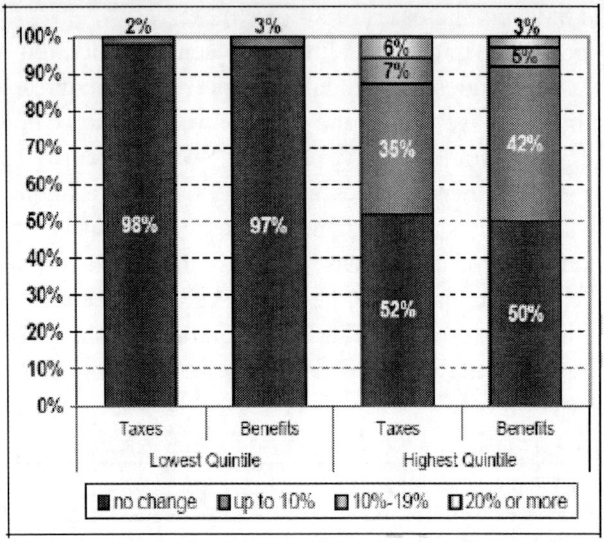

Source: CRS calculations using the Urban Institute's Dynasim microsimulation model.

Figure 4. Share of Beneficiaries in 2035 with Higher Payroll Taxes or Benefits Compared with Current Law If the Taxable Earnings Base Is Eliminated, by Highest and Lowest Quintile

Changes by Income Group

The impact of eliminating the taxable wage base on payroll taxes paid varies significantly by income group.[17] The overwhelming majority (98%) of beneficiaries in 2035 in the lowest income quintile would pay no additional taxes over their lifetime (Figure 4). Few in this group would receive benefit increases if the cap were removed. Under this proposal only 3% of beneficiaries in the lowest income category would receive benefit increases, and the increase would be for less than 10%.

The story is different for higher-income beneficiaries. Roughly one-half of those in the highest income quintile are estimated to have had tax increases over their lifetimes relative to current law. Whereas 35% of beneficiaries in the top quintile would see their lifetime taxes rise by less than 10%, some (7%) would see their taxes rise between 10% and 19% and some (6%) would see their taxes rise 20% or more. Beneficiaries in the highest income groups would also see the largest change in their benefits if the taxable wage base were removed. One-half of beneficiaries in the top fifth of the income distribution in 2035 would have an increase in benefits relative to current law. In this highest quintile, 42% would have benefit increases of less than 10%, some (5%) would have benefit increases of 10%-19% and a few (3%) would have benefit increases of 20% or more.

Changes by Gender

Because the majority of workers who earn above the taxable wage base in a given year are men (Table A-3 and described above), men would be more likely to pay higher payroll taxes than women if the taxable wage base were eliminated. Among men who receive benefits in 2035, more than one in four would pay higher payroll taxes over the course of their lifetimes (Figure 5). Twenty percent of male beneficiaries would have a tax increase of less than 10%, but 7% would see their lifetime tax contributions increase by more than 10%. If the taxable earnings base was removed, one in four men would receive higher benefits.

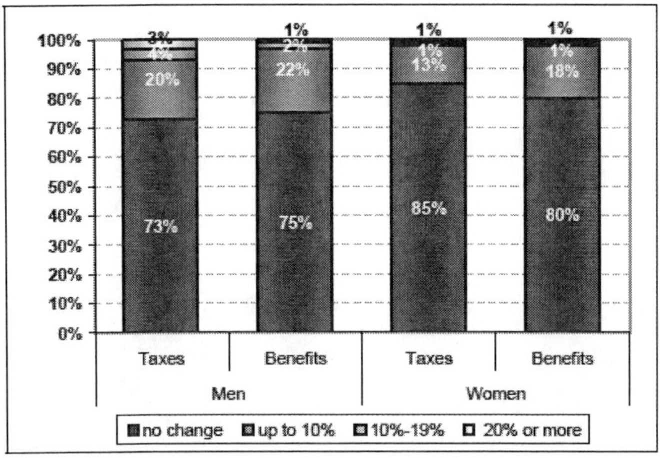

Source: CRS calculations using the Urban Institute's Dynasim microsimulation model.

Figure 5. Share of Male and Female Beneficiaries in 2035 with Higher Payroll Taxes or Benefits Compared with Current Law If the Taxable Earnings Base Is Eliminated, by Gender

The majority of the men affected (22% of all male beneficiaries) would see a small increase in benefits, but 3% of all men would have benefits increase by more than 10%. In contrast, only 15% of women who receive benefits in 2035 would have paid any additional payroll taxes over the course of their lives. Of these women, only 2% would have an increase of more than 10%. Because many women receive benefits based on their spouses' earnings, the share of women who would see a rise in benefits is higher than the share that would pay additional taxes. Although the benefits of one in five female beneficiaries in 2035 would rise, for most it would be a small increase of less than 10%.

Table 2. Impact on the Social Security Trust Funds of Raising or Eliminating the Social Security Taxable Earnings Base

	Year the Trust Funds Are Exhausted	75-Year Actuarial Balance (as % of taxable payroll)	Percentage of 75-Year Shortfall Met
No change to current law	2041	-1.92	
Option 1: Make 90% of the earnings subject to the payroll tax and credit them for benefit purposes (phased in 2006-2015)	2044	-1.09	43%
Option 2: Make all earnings subject to the payroll tax and credit them for benefit purposes (beginning in 2006)	na[a]	-0.10	95%
	Year the Trust Funds Are Exhausted	**75-Year Actuarial Balance (as % of taxable payroll)**	**Percentage of 75-Year Shortfall Met**
Option 3: Make all earnings subject to the payroll tax but retain the cap for benefit calculations (beginning in 2006)	na[a]	0.28	115%

Sources: Social Security Administration, Memorandum, dated August 10, 2005.
Notes: All calculations use the intermediate assumptions of the 2005 Trustees Report.
a. Solvent beyond 75-year estimate.

Table 3. Revenue Impact of Raising the Social Security Taxable Earnings Base

	Taxable Wage Base (dollars)	Total Change in Revenues (billions of dollars)	
Year	2008	2008-2012	2008-2017
Tax 92% of earnings	250,000	+284.7	+682.7
Tax 91% of earnings	214,000	+253.5	+604.3
Tax 90% of earnings	186,000	+221.1	+524.4

Source: *Joint Committee on Taxation, 2007.*

Impact on the Social Security Trust Funds

Under the assumptions of the 2009 Trustees Report, the actuaries at the Social Security Administration calculate that it would take an immediate increase in combined payroll taxes of 2.0% of taxable payroll (from 12.40% to 14.40%) to achieve solvency over the next 75 years.[18] Without this increase or other changes to the system, the 2009 Trustees Report projected that the OASDI Trust Funds would be exhausted in 2041. The actuaries at SSA have estimated the impact on the Trust Funds of three options to change the benefit and contribution base which are described below.

Option 1: Cover 90% of Earnings and Pay Higher Benefits

One proposal would slowly raise the taxable wage base for both employers and employees to cover 90% of all earnings and credit these taxes to allow individuals to receive correspondingly higher benefits. In 2006, it was estimated that a cap of $171,600 would roughly cover 90% of wages.[19] Under this option, benefits at retirement for high earners would also rise. These changes would have a net positive impact on the Social Security Trust Funds (Table 2). Raising the wage base to 90% would eliminate 43% of the long-range financial shortfall—extending the Trust Funds' exhaustion date to 2044. To achieve solvency for the full 75-year projection period under this option, the total payroll tax rate would have to be raised by an additional 1.09 percentage points (from 12.40% to 13.49%) or other policy changes would have to be made to cover the shortfall.[20]

Option 2: Cover All Earnings and Pay Higher Benefits

If the earnings base was completely eliminated for both employers and employees so that all earnings were taxed, 95% of the projected financial shortfall in the Social Security program would be eliminated. To achieve solvency for the full 75-year projection period under this option, the total payroll tax rate would have to be raised by an additional 0.1 percentage points (from 12.4% to 12.5%) or other policy changes would have to be made to cover the shortfall.

Under this scenario high earners would pay higher taxes but also receive higher benefits. However, the net benefit to the Trust Funds is positive as $5 in additional revenue would provide only $1 in additional benefits (on average over their 75-year valuation period). Annual Social Security benefit payments would be much higher than today's maximum of $25,440. A worker who paid taxes on earnings of $400,000 each year would get a benefit of approximately $6,000 a month or $72,000 a year—a replacement rate of 18%—while someone with lifetime earnings of $1 million a year would get a monthly Social Security benefit of approximately $13,500 a month or $162,000 a year—a replacement rate of 16.2%.[21]

Option 3: Cover All Earnings and Pay No Additional Benefits

Finally, if the base was completely eliminated for both employers and employees so that all earnings were taxed, but those earnings did not count toward benefits, solvency would be restored to Social Security. The increased revenue would eliminate 115% of the projected shortfall and the program would have a projected surplus equal to .28% of taxable payroll. Under this scenario, the payroll tax rate could be immediately *lowered* from 12.40% to 12.12% and the system would remain solvent for the next 75 years. However, the traditional link between the level of wages that is taxed and the level of wages that counts toward benefits would be broken.

Impact on Federal Revenue

Raising the taxable earnings base would lead to an increase in total federal revenues. The Joint Committee on Taxation has estimated that raising the wage base to 90% of earnings, to $186,000 in 2008, would generate $221 billion in additional revenue over the five-year budget window of 2008-2012 (Table 3).[22] Over 10 years, the policy would generate more than $524 billion.

Raising the payroll tax base to cover an additional 1%-2% of income (above the 90% level) would generate $32 billion-$64 billion more over five years and $80 billion-$158 billion more over 10 years.

Impact on Workers' and Employers' Behavior

The reaction of high-earning workers and their employers to raising or removing the taxable earnings base is unknown and was not taken into consideration in the above estimates of the distributional, trust fund, and revenue impacts.

Workers who earn more than the cap would have a reduced incentive to work as their after-tax earnings will fall.[23] However, whether these individuals would significantly reduce the amount they work is a matter of debate.[24] Each worker would face a decision between the reduced earnings and the additional leisure time, based on the worker's individual preferences. Workers who have earnings above the current base would also have an incentive to change the form of their compensation (e.g., from earnings to fringe benefits) to avoid paying additional payroll taxes.[25]

The impact of raising the base on employers of high-income earners is also unknown. Employers contribute 6.2% of workers' wages up to the taxable wage base toward Social Security. If employers are unable to pass along the higher tax costs to workers in the form of reduced earnings, their overall labor costs will increase. Employers may react by raising prices to consumers, reducing other non-wage forms of compensation such as health benefits or pensions, or reducing the number of workers.

LEGISLATION IN THE 111TH CONGRESS

One bill has been introduced in the 111th Congress to change the taxable wage base. H.R. 1863, introduced by Representative Wexler, would require workers and employers to contribute 3% of earnings above the taxable wage base, and self-employed individuals to contribute 6%. Earnings above the taxable wage base would not be credited for benefit computation purposes.

ARGUMENTS FOR AND AGAINST RAISING OR ELIMINATING THE BASE

Some of the general arguments for and against changing the Social Security taxable earnings base follow.

Arguments For

The major critique about the Social Security base is that it creates a regressive tax structure. Workers earning less than the base have a greater proportion of earnings taxed than workers whose earnings exceed it. In 2008, someone with annual earnings of $30,000 pays $1,860 in Social Security taxes, or 6.2% of his or her earnings (ignoring the employer share of the tax).

However, because the tax is levied on only the first $106,800 in earnings, someone earning $200,000 a year pays $6,622 or 3% of his or her earnings.

Supporters of changing the wage base point out that only 6% of workers have earnings above the base in any given year. However, because of rising earnings inequality, the amount of their earnings that escapes taxation has risen from 12% to 15% since 1991, and is projected to continue to rise through 2014. They therefore contend that the current tax structure favors a small group of the more well-off workers in society.

They also point out that the overall employee tax rate rose from 6.13% in 1980 to 7.65% in 1990 (counting the Medicare portion)—or by 25%—and assert that this increase is one of the main reasons for a disproportionate rise in the aggregate federal tax burden on lower- and middle- income people over that decade.[26] They further maintain that for most workers, Social Security and Medicare taxes (counting the employer share, which they view as foregone wages) are now greater than their income taxes.

Supporters argue that subjecting a larger percentage of earnings to the payroll tax would also adjust for the higher life expectancies of high earners.[27] On average, people with more education and higher earnings live longer than those with lower earnings and less education and this difference has been growing over time. The impact on the Social Security program is that these individuals receive benefits for more years over their lifetimes making the system less progressive.[28] They claim that raising the taxable wage base would make a reasonable adjustment for the faster-than-average life expectancy gains among high earners.

Thus, supporters of changing the base argue that raising or eliminating the base not only would be more fair, but also that Social Security's projected long-range financing problems could be substantially alleviated or, alternatively, that the payroll tax rate could be reduced without causing a loss of revenue to the system. It is estimated that almost $100 billion in revenue to the Social Security program would be generated annually by taxing all earnings, and if such revenues were not used to lower the tax rate, they would reduce the government's outstanding debt and eliminate about 95% of Social Security's long-range deficit.

Among supporters of changing the current base, there is disagreement regarding how high the base should be raised or if other changes should be made to tax income above the base. Several proposals would not eliminate the base entirely but raise it to cover 90% of taxable wages, restoring the level that was set in the 1977 amendments to the Social Security Act. Others have claimed that increasing the base to 90% would be a large tax increase for those who earn between the current base and the new level, but would have little impact on the share of taxes paid by individuals with the highest earnings.[29] Other options would be to remove the cap completely over the base, but lower the tax rate on those higher earnings[30] or tax employers and employees at different rates above the current base. Others have called for broadening the sources of income that are taxed beyond earnings.[31] Proponents of these ideas argue that they would close a significant portion of Social Security's long-range deficit without subjecting upper-middle income individuals to sizeable increases in their marginal tax rates.

Arguments Against

Those who support keeping the base as it is point out that while the structure of the payroll tax may be regressive, it is offset by the progressive calculation of benefits.

They further maintain that its critics fail to take into account the effect of other tax and transfer programs targeted to low-earners. They point out that mitigating the Social Security tax bite was part of the motivation for creating the earned income tax credit (EITC), which provides an income tax credit on earnings up to $41,646 in 2008 for married workers with two or more children (up to $15,880 for married workers without children). They also point out that low- income families receive a greater share of government transfer payments that are not subject to Social Security payroll taxes. They argue that the combination of these factors mitigates the flat- rate nature of the tax at lower earnings levels, and that for most other workers the tax is proportional (because it is flat-rate). It is only at the upper end of the income spectrum that it takes on a regressive appearance.

Critics also argue that raising the cap will serve as a disincentive to work and could serve as a drain on the economy. [32] Because additional work effort would generate less after-tax income, supporters claim that workers faced with this higher marginal rate would either reduce their hours or avoid the tax by changing the form of their compensation.

From another perspective, some—who might otherwise espouse progressive taxation—support raising the base but not eliminating it. Having a cap makes Social Security seem less like general purpose taxation. They argue that the system needs support from people of all earnings levels, and that the larger benefits that high earners would receive would represent a poor return for the higher taxes they would pay. Moreover, regardless of the money's worth issue, some question the wisdom of paying large benefits to well-to-do people. They argue that the purpose of the program is to provide a floor of protection for retirement, not large benefits for those who can save on their own. They contend that eliminating the base would raise public cynicism about a publicly financed system that pays enormous benefits to people who already are well off.

APPENDIX. TAXABLE EARNINGS BASES AND WORKER INCOME: DETAILED TABLES

Table A-1. Social Security and Medicare Tax Rates and Taxable Earnings Bases, 1937-20 10

Year	Tax Rates			Maximum taxable earnings for Social Security and HI	Percentage of workers with earnings below Social Security base	Percentage of covered earnings below Social Security base
	Social Security[a]	HI[a]	Self-employed (Social Security and HI combined)			
1937	1.000	—	—	$3,000	96.9	92.0

1940	1.000	—	—	3,000	96.6	92.4
1945	1.000	—	—	3,000	86.3	87.9
1950	1.500	—	—	3,000	71.1	79.7
1951	1.500	—	2.25	3,600	75.5	81.1
1952	1.500	—	2.25	3,600	72.1	80.5
1953	1.500	—	2.25	3,600	68.8	78.5
1954	2.000	—	3.0	3,600	68.4	77.7
1955	2.000	—	3.0	4,200	74.4	80.3
1956	2.000	—	3.0	4,200	71.6	78.8
1957	2.250	—	3.375	4,200	70.1	77.5
1958	2.250	—	3.375	4,200	69.4	76.4
1959	2.500	—	3.75	4,800	73.3	79.3
1960	3.000	—	4.5	4,800	72.0	78.1
1961	3.000	—	4.5	4,800	70.8	77.4
1962	3.125	—	4.7	4,800	68.8	75.8
1963	3.625	—	5.4	4,800	67.5	74.6
1964	3.625	—	5.4	4,800	65.5	72.8
1965	3.625	—	5.4	4,800	63.9	71.3
1966	3.850	0.35	6.15	6,600	75.8	80.0
1967	3.900	0.5	6.4	6,600	73.6	78.1
1968	3.800	0.6	6.4	7,800	78.6	81.7
1969	4.200	0.6	6.9	7,800	75.5	80.1
1970	4.200	0.6	6.9	7,800	74.0	78.2
1971	4.600	0.6	7.5	7,800	71.7	76.3
1972	4.600	0.6	7.5	9,000	75.0	78.3
1973	4.850	1.0	8.0	10,800	79.7	81.8
1974	4.950	0.9	7.9	13,200	84.9	85.3
1975	4.950	0.9	7.9	14,100	84.9	84.4
1976	4.950	0.9	7.9	15,300	85.1	84.3
1977	4.950	0.9	7.9	16,500	85.2	85.0
1978	5.050	1.0	8.1	17,700	84.6	83.8
1979	5.080	1.05	8.1	22,900	90.0	87.3
1980	5.080	1.05	8.1	25,900	91.2	88.9
1981	5.350	1.3	9.3	29,700	92.4	89.2
1982	5.400	1.3	9.35	32,400	92.9	90.0
1983	5.400	1.3	9.35	35,700	93.7	90.0
1984	5.700	1.3	14.0	37,800	93.6	89.3
1985	5.700	1.35	14.1	39,600	93.5	88.9

Table A-1 (Continued)						
1986	5.700	1.45	14.3	42,000	93.8	88.6
1987	5.700	1.45	14.3	43,800	93.9	87.6
1988	6.060	1.45	15.02	45,000	93.5	85.8
1989	6.060	1.45	15.02	48,000	93.8	86.8
1990	6.200	1.45	15.3	51,300	94.3	87.2
1991	6.200	1.45	15.3	53,400 (HI-125,000)	94.4	87.8
1992	6.200	1.45	15.3	55,500 (HI-130,200)	94.3	86.8
1993	6.200	1.45	15.3	57,600 (HI-135,000)	94.4	87.2
1994	6.200	1.45	15.3	60,600[a] (HI-no limit)	94.6	87.1
1995	6.200	1.45	15.3	61,200 (HI-no limit)	94.2	85.8
1996	6.200	1.45	15.3	62,700 (HI-no limit)	93.9	85.7
1997	6.200	1.45	15.3	65,400 (HI-no limit)	93.8	85.1
1998	6.200	1.45	15.3	68,400 (HI-no limit)	93.7	84.5
1999	6.200	1.45	15.3	72,600 (HI-no limit)	93.9	83.9
2000	6.200	1.45	15.3	76,200 (HI-no limit)	93.8	83.2
2001	6.200	1.45	15.3	80,400 (HI-no limit)	94.0	84.7
2002	6.200	1.45	15.3	84,900 (HI-no limit)	94.6	86.1

2003	6.200	1.45	15.3	87,000 (HI-no limit)	94.5	85.9
2004	6.200	1.45	15.3	87,900 (HI-no limit)	94.1	84.8
2005	6.200	1.45	15.3	90,000 (HI-no limit)	94.0b	84.2b
2006	6.200	1.45	15.3	94,200 (HI-no limit)	94.0b	83.6b
2007	6.200	1.45	15.3	97,500 (HI-no limit)	93.9b	83.1b
2008	6.200	1.45	15.3	102,000 (HI-no limit)	Not yet known	84.1b
2009	6.200	1.45	15.3	106,800 (HI-no limit)	Not yet known	Not yet known
2009	6.200	1.45	15.3	106,800 (HI-no limit)	Not yet known	Not yet known

Source: Social Security Bulletin, *Annual Statistical Supplement, 2009* at http://www.ssa.gov/policy/docs/statcomps/ supplement/2009.

a. Same for employer except 1984—employees received 0.3% credit (not reflected above). Various credits also applied to self-employed (not reflected above) for 1984-1989 period.

b. Estimates.

Table A-2. The Number and Percentage of Covered Workers with Social Security Taxable Earnings over the Taxable Earnings Base of $90,000, by State, 2005

State	Total Number of Covered Workers With Social Security Taxable Earnings	Number and Share of Covered Workers with Social Security Taxable Earnings Above the Taxable Earnings Base	
		Number of Workers	Percentage of Workers
U.S. Total	154,603,000	9,509,000	6.2

Table A-2 (Continued)

Alabama	2,292,200	87,400	3.8
Alaska	373,600	20,900	5.6
Arizona	2,859,100	164,100	5.7
Arkansas	1,440,100	39,300	2.7
California	16,561,300	1,466,000	8.9
Colorado	2,370,400	160,000	6.7
Connecticut	1,927,200	195,900	10.2
District of Columbia	353,100	42,600	12.1
Delaware	500,000	28,600	5.7
Florida	9,114,900	439,600	4.8
Georgia	4,536,300	259,500	5.7
Hawaii	705,900	29,600	4.2
Idaho	757,800	27,200	3.6
Illinois	6,436,200	456,500	7.1
Indiana	3,551,900	141,500	4.0
Iowa	1,701,300	58,400	3.4
Kansas	1,525,500	66,600	4.4
Kentucky	2,114,500	73,400	3.5
Louisiana	2,066,900	86,300	4.2
Maine	762,200	25,700	3.4
Maryland	3,117,500	282,700	9.1
Massachusetts	3,381,200	326,900	9.7
Michigan	5,306,700	314,700	5.9
Minnesota	3,047,000	178,500	5.9
Mississippi	1,369,100	35,300	2.6
Missouri	3,083,300	125,200	4.1
Montana	537,600	15,200	2.8
Nebraska	1,031,000	35,000	3.4
Nevada	1,188,100	54,600	4.6
New Hampshire	797,400	57,300	7.2
New Jersey	4,702,000	539,500	11.5
New Mexico	911,200	34,500	3.8
New York	9,877,100	838,900	8.5
North Carolina	4,554,300	217,200	4.8
North Dakota	386,200	10,700	2.8
Ohio	5,811,500	286,900	4.9
Oklahoma	1,816,400	54,700	3.0
Oregon	1,895,700	95,300	5.0
Pennsylvania	6,652,800	378,500	5.7
Rhode Island	611,000	38,400	6.3
South Carolina	2,189,600	79,000	3.6

South Dakota	476,500	9,900	2.1
Tennessee	3,144,600	136,800	4.4
Texas	10,657,000	663,100	6.2
Utah	1,250,800	49,600	4.0
Vermont	415,800	15,800	3.8
Virginia	4,194,200	334,500	8.0
Washington	3,316,600	219,800	6.6
West Virginia	875,000	25,400	2.9
Wisconsin	3,149,700	129,500	4.1
Wyoming	315,800	10,700	3.4

Source: Custom tabulation based on the Continuous Work History Sample Files. Data extracted as of January 2007. Table provided by SSA, Office of Policy, Office of Research, Evaluation and Statistics.

Table A-3. Number and Percentage of Workers Above the Taxable Earnings Base of $97,500 by Type of Earnings and Sex, 2007

	Number[a] (in thousands)	Percentage of Group in Total	Percent of Group Above the Taxable Maximum
All workers	10,210	100%	6%
Men	7,813	77%	9%
Women	2,399	23%	3%
All wage and salary workers	9,420	92%	6%
Men	7,168	70%	9%
Women	2,253	22%	3%
All self-employed	790	8%	5%
Men	645	6%	6%
Women	146	2%	2%

Source: Social Security Bulletin, *Annual Statistical Supplement*, 2009 at http://www.ssa.gov/policy/docs/statcomps/supplement/2009. (CRS calculations based on 2007 estimates from tables, 4.B1,4.B4, 4.B7, and 4B.9).

a. Workers with earnings in both wage and salary employment and self-employment are counted in each type of employment but only once in the total.

End Notes

[1] The reason for the two-year lag in reflecting increases in average wages in the taxable earnings base is that average wages for the year immediately prior to the year of the increase simply are not known in time.

[2] The maximum for a worker was to be $3,000 per year per employer, so that, under the original legislation enacted in 1935, someone could have paid tax on more than $3,000 in earnings per year (and received benefits from all such wages) if they worked for more than one employer.

[3] The same maximum taxable amount was set for the self-employed when they were covered in 1951 and for the Disability Insurance (DI) portion of the tax when it was first levied in 1957.

[4] Social Security Administration, Office of the Chief Actuary, *Social Security Program Fact Sheet,* available at http://www.ssa.gov/OACT/FACTS/index.html.Some workers (approximately 4%) are exempt from Social Security payroll taxes and are therefore not "covered" by Social Security. From this point forward, all references to earnings are "covered" earnings and workers are "covered" workers. For a listing of workers who are exempt from Social Security taxes, see CRS Report 94-28, *Social Security and Medicare Taxes and Premiums: Fact Sheet,* by Dawn Nuschler.

[5] $106,800 x 6.2% = $6,622 and $106,800 x 12.4% = $13,243.

[6] The Social Security benefit formula calculates benefits based on a worker's highest 35 years of earnings.

[7]Social Security Administration, 2009 Fact Sheet, available at *http://www.ssa.gov/ pressoffice/factsheets/* colafacts2009.pdf.

[8] At least some of this decline and subsequent increase in the ratio after 2000 is believed to be due to stock option activity surrounding the stock market bubble in 2000 and is not likely to recur. (SSA, *2005 OASDI Trustees Report.*)

[9] Note that the years denoted for **Table A-1**, **Table A-2**, and **Table A-3** differ slightly due to differences in availability of data.

[10] Social Security Administration, *Annual Statistical Supplement 2009,* http://www.ssa.gov/policy/docs/statcomps/ supplement/2009/4b.html#table4.b1. (Hereafter referred to as SSA Statistical Supplement, 2009.)

[11] The Urban Institute's Dynamic Simulation of Income Model (Dynasim) is a computer model that uses survey data to project earnings, demographic changes, retirement income, and Social Security benefits through the year 2050. For more information about the model, how it works, and how to interpret results, see CRS Report RL33 840, *Options to Address Social Security Solvency and Their Impact on Beneficiaries: Results from the Dynasim Microsimulation Model,* by Dawn Nuschler et al.

[12] SSA Statistical Supplement, 2009.

[13] The share of the population affected by this policy is influenced by the way the Dynasim model projects an individual's earnings. There is a significant amount of year-to-year variation in the projection of each individual's earnings.

[14] The Dynasim model projections are consistent with current data on wage inequality. In 2004, the top 1% of earners were paid 11% of aggregate earnings (source: CRS analysis of the March 2005 Current Population Survey).

[15] There is precedent for this proposal. When the hospital insurance (HI) tax was levied in 1966 the maximum taxable amount was set the same as for Social Security. As part of the Omnibus Budget Reconciliation Act of 1993 (P.L. 103- 66), the HI base was removed.

[16] CRS estimates of the impact of this and other reform proposals, including raising the base to cover 90% of taxable earnings, are also available based on beneficiaries' socioeconomic status (including ethnicity, education, and marital status). (CRS Report RL33 841, *Options*

to Address Social Security Solvency and Their Impact on Beneficiaries: Results from the Dynasim Microsimulation Model—Detailed Distributional Tables, by Dawn Nuschler et al.)

[17] Note that the income groups are defined in 2035 using family income after an individual claims disability, retirement, survivor, or spousal benefits. Thus, some low income beneficiaries are affected by the policy if they earned above the taxable wage base at any point in their careers.

[18] The projections in this section were done using the assumptions of the 2005 Trustees Report to match the estimates in Table 4, which are the most recent estimates available for these options.

[19] Social Security Administration, *Estimated Financial Effects of "A Nonpartisan Approach to Reforming Social Security - A Proposal Developed by Jeffrey Liebman, Maya MacGuineas and Andrew Samwick "—INFORMATION*, Memorandum, dated November 17, 2005, http://www.ssa.gov/OACT/solvency/Liebman_20051117.pdf.

[20] Social Security Administration, *Estimated OASDI Long-Range Financial Effects of Several Provisions Requested by the Social Security Advisory Board*, Memorandum, dated August 10, 2005, available at http://www.ssa.gov/OACT/ solvency/provisions/index.html.

[21] Calculations are for 2005 from Reno and Lavery, *Options to Balance Social Security Funds*, February 2005. Benefits this high would be extremely rare as few individuals earn above the taxable wage base for their entire career.

[22] Congressional Budget Office, *Budget Options, Revenue Option 39: Increase the Upper Limit for Earnings Subject to the Social Security Payroll Tax*, February 2007, at http://www.cbo.gov.

Note that the estimates by the actuaries at the Social Security Administration (SSA) and the Joint Committee on Taxation (JCT) differ slightly due to different assumptions. SSA assumes the maximum wage base will be adjusted each year to keep taxable wages at a constant percent of wages whereas the JCT assumes it will be a one-time increase with adjustments only for inflation thereafter. JCT estimates also account for the effects on all sources of revenue, including changes to income taxes and Medicare taxes.

[23] The response by high earners may depend on whether the wage base is raised slightly or completely eliminated.

[24] For a more detailed discussion of this debate, see CRS Report RL33 943, *Increasing the Social Security Payroll Tax Base: Options and Effects on Tax Burdens*, by Thomas L. Hungerford.

[25] See Martin Sullivan, "Budget Magic and the Social Security Tax Cap," *Tax Notes*, March 14, 2005.

[26] See CRS Report RL32693, *Distribution of the Tax Burden Across Individuals: An Overview*, by Jane G. Gravelle and Maxim Shvedov.

[27] See Peter A. Diamond and Peter R. Orzag, *Saving Social Security: A Balanced Approach*, Brookings Institution, 2004.

[28] The Social Security benefit formula is thought to be progressive in that the monthly benefits of low-wage earners replace a greater proportion of their earnings than do the monthly benefits of high-wage earners.

[29] For a study of how the effective tax rates paid by different income groups would change under such a proposal, see CRS Report RL33943, *Increasing the Social Security Payroll Tax Base: Options and Effects on Tax Burdens*, by Thomas L. Hungerford.

[30] Robert C. Posen, "PIN Money," *Wall Street Journal*, January 9, 2007.

[31] Citizens for Tax Justice, *An Analysis of Eliminating the Cap on Earnings Subject to the Social Security Tax and Related Issues*, November 30, 2006, at *http://www.ctj.org/pdf /socialsecuritytaxearningscapnov2006.pdf.*

[32] See D. Mark Wilson, *Removing the Social Security's Tax Cap on Wages Would Do More Harm Than Good*, The Heritage Foundation, October 18, 2001.

In: Social Security: Background, Issues and... ISBN: 978-1-61761-469-9
Editors: Jacob T. Álvarez

Chapter 6

INCREASING THE SOCIAL SECURITY PAYROLL TAX BASE: OPTIONS AND EFFECTS ON TAX BURDENS

Thomas L. Hungerford

SUMMARY

According to the Social Security Trustees, assets in the two Social Security trust funds will be exhausted by 2037, and, thereafter, Social Security payroll tax revenues will cover about three-quarters of promised benefits. Over the past decade several proposals have been put forward which could help to close the Social Security program's long-term financing gap. One proposal would increase the Social Security payroll tax base so that 90% of covered earnings are taxable— the same proportion as in 1982. This policy would increase the payroll taxes paid by higher- earning workers and not affect workers earning less than the current Social Security maximum taxable limit, which is $106,800 in 2010.

Some analysts have proposed raising the Social Security payroll tax base and reducing the payroll tax rate. This policy would increase the taxes paid by higher-earning workers and reduce taxes paid by low- and middle-income workers. This policy proposal could raise revenue for the Social Security program or be revenue neutral.

Although the legislated Social Security payroll tax rate is 12.4%, the average Social Security payroll tax is slightly progressive throughout the bottom 80% of the income distribution in that lower-income families pay a lower proportion of income in payroll taxes than higher-income families. At the higher-income levels—the top 20%—the payroll tax is regressive in that the proportion of income paid in payroll taxes falls as income rises. The richest 1% of American families pay a smaller proportion of their income in payroll taxes than the poorest 20% of families.

Three policy options, which raise the payroll tax base, are examined; two of the policies also provide tax relief to low- and middle-income workers. Each of the three policies reduces the regressivity of the payroll tax at the upper end of the income distribution. Currently, less than 10% of families contain a worker earning more than the maximum taxable limit. Consequently, over 90% of families would be unaffected by increasing the maximum taxable limit. And if this change were combined with a payroll tax rate reduction, over 90% of families would pay lower payroll taxes.

It has been argued that the revenue increases from raising the payroll tax base would be significantly less than expected because of indirect behavioral changes by workers. These predicted behavioral effects would reduce taxable earnings, the proportion of family income subject to payroll taxes, and tax revenue. But recent research raises doubts concerning this position and suggests these behavioral effects would likely be negligible.

The payroll tax for Social Security and Medicare is the largest federal tax many lower- income families pay. The Congressional Budget Office (CBO) estimates that the poorest 20% of U.S. households paid about 8.5% of their income on social insurance payroll taxes in 2006.[1] In contrast, these lower-income households paid negative income taxes because of the refundable earned income and child tax credits. Indeed, a justification for the earned income credit (EIC) is "to provide work incentives and relief from income and Social Security taxes to low-income families who might otherwise need large welfare payments."[2]

The tax rate under current law on covered earnings is 12.4% for Social Security and 2.9% for Medicare.[3] Half of the tax rate is paid by the employee and the other half by the employer; the self-employed are responsible for the entire amount.[4] The tax rate for Social Security applies only on covered earnings below the maximum taxable limit, which is $106,800 for 2010.[5] The Medicare tax rate applies to all covered earnings.

The Social Security Trustees project that the assets in the two Social Security trust funds will be exhausted in 2037, and after that, Social Security payroll tax revenue will cover about three- quarters of promised benefits.[6] To help close Social Security's long-term financing gap, some analysts have proposed increasing the Social Security tax base by raising the maximum taxable limit so that 90% of aggregate covered earnings are taxable (the percentage in 1982).[7] CBO estimates that the maximum taxable limit would have to increase to $186,000 in 2008, almost double the current limit, so that 90% of covered earnings are taxable. It is estimated that this policy could increase payroll tax revenues by $503.4 billion over the 2010-2019 period.[8] Since 1982, the ratio of taxable earnings to covered earnings has fallen from 90%, reaching 82.7% in 2007.

Although most analysts advocate raising the maximum taxable limit to increase revenues for the Social Security program, some would use the increased revenues for other purposes. For example, one analyst suggested reducing the payroll tax rate and keeping it revenue-neutral by raising the maximum taxable limit.[9] This change would provide payroll tax relief to low- and middle-income workers.

This chapter examines changes in the distribution of the tax burden of three policies involving raising the Social Security maximum taxable limit.

TAXABLE AND COVERED EARNINGS

The portion of Social Security-covered earnings subject to the payroll tax has fluctuated since its inception. Taxable earnings as a percentage of covered earnings was 92.4% in 1940 and dropped as low as 7 1.3% in 1965. The trend in this percentage since 1950 is displayed in Figure 1. Prior to 1972, the Social Security maximum taxable limit was updated periodically by Congress, which contributed to the dramatic and abrupt fluctuations in the 1950s and 1960s. After 1972, the maximum taxable limit was automatically updated as annual average earnings increased, which moderated the fluctuations somewhat. In response to Social Security funding problems, the 1977 amendments to the Social Security Act increased the Social Security tax base by raising the maximum taxable limit so that 90% of covered earnings were taxable by 1982. This change explains the increase in the proportion of covered earnings that are taxable from 84% in 1976 to 90% in 1982. After 1982, the maximum taxable limit was automatically updated as annual average earnings increased.

Although the maximum taxable limit is updated annually in response to increases in average wages, the proportion of covered earnings subject to the payroll tax is not constant—it has fallen since 1983. A primary reason is an increase in wage inequality. Wages have become more unequally distributed since the early 1 980s, mostly due to wage gains at the top of the income distribution. [10] Consequently, a larger share of earnings of high-wage workers will be above the maximum taxable limit.

THE DISTRIBUTION OF TAX BURDENS

The distribution of tax burdens is simulated for three policy options, two of which have been proposed by various policy analysts. The base year for the simulation is 2008, the last year for which appropriate data is available.[11] The policy options compared in this chapter are:

- **Policy Option 1**. This policy would increase the maximum taxable limit to $186,000 (up from the 2008 limit of $102,000), which is the maximum taxable limit required so that 90% of covered earnings would have been subject to the payroll tax in 2007. The additional tax revenues are targeted to help close Social Security's projected long-term financing gap. Consequently, the payroll tax rate remains at 12.4%.
- **Policy Option 2**. This policy would also raise the maximum taxable limit to $186,000 but reduce the payroll tax rate to 11.4% so payroll tax revenues remain unchanged. In essence, the additional payroll tax revenues from increasing the maximum taxable limit are used to offset the reduction in the payroll tax rate.
- **Policy Option 3**. This policy option would raise the maximum taxable limit to $186,000. However, half of the additional revenue is targeted to reduce the projected long-term financing gap and the other half is used to offset a payroll tax rate reduction. The payroll tax rate is reduced to 11.9%.

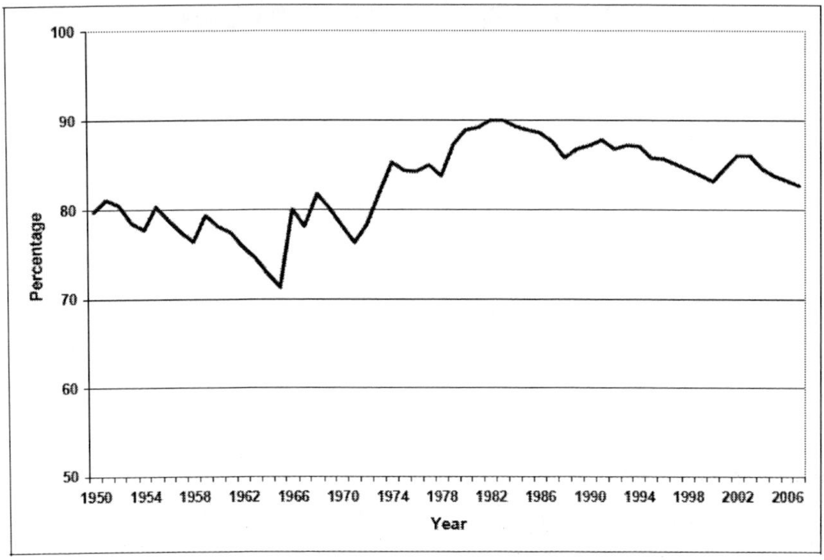

Source: Social Security Administration, 2007 Annual Statistical Supplement to the Social Security Bulletin, Table 4.B1.

Figure 1 . Taxable Earnings as a Percentage of Social Security Covered Earnings, 1950-2007

Simulation results of the average Social Security tax rate for families with workers in different parts of the income distribution are reported in Table 1. The average tax rate is the total payroll tax (employee and employer shares) of each worker in the family and divided by total family income. Total family income includes wages, dividends, farm income, retirement income, royalties, and government cash transfers, among others. It does not include capital gains and in- kind government transfers such as food stamps and housing assistance. The average tax rate is reported for all families, each income quintile (20% of families), the richest 10% of families, the richest 5%, and the richest 1% of families.[12]

The first column of numbers in Table 1 shows the average tax rate under current law. The average tax rate for all families is 9.7%, which is less than the 12.4% statutory payroll tax rate on earnings. This occurs because only earnings are subject to the payroll tax while income from other sources is not. In addition, only the first $102,000 earned in 2008 was subject to the payroll tax while earnings above $102,000 were exempt.

Table 1. Average Social Security Payroll Tax Rates

		90% of Covered Payroll is Taxable		
	Current	**Policy Option 1**	**Policy Option 2**	**Policy Option 3**
All	9.66%	10.34%	9.50%	9.93%
Quintile 1	10.40	10.40	9.55	9.98
Quintile 2	10.55	10.55	9.69	10.13
Quintile 3	10.84	10.84	9.96	10.40
Quintile 4	10.97	11.03	10.14	10.59
Quintile 5	8.53	9.84	9.04	9.44
Top 10%	7.43	9.21	8.46	8.84
Top 5%	6.08	8.30	7.62	7.96
Top 1%	3.73	6.24	5.73	5.99

Source: Author's analysis of the March 2009 Current Population Survey.
Note: The sample includes only families that contain at least one worker.

The average tax rate, however, varies across the income distribution. Families in the poorest income quintile (that is, the poorest 20% of families) have an average tax rate of 10.4%. The average tax rate slightly increases in moving from the poorest quintile to the fourth quintile. Throughout the bottom 80% of the income distribution, the Social Security payroll tax is slightly progressive in that higher-income families pay a larger proportion of their income in payroll taxes than lower-income families.

The average tax rate for families in the richest income quintile, however, is 8.5%.[13] The rate falls in moving up through the upper part of the income distribution. The richest 10% of families pay a smaller share of income in payroll taxes than the poorest 20%, while the share of the richest 1% is about a third that of the poorest 20%. Above the 80th percentile, the payroll tax is a regressive tax in that the average tax rate falls as income rises.[14]

The second column of numbers shows the simulated average tax rates for policy option 1— raising the maximum taxable limit and maintaining the current legislated tax rate. For all families, the average tax rate rises by almost 0.7 percentage points (a 7% increase) to reach over 10%. This policy option, however, only affects workers whose earnings are above $102,000. Families in the bottom two income quintiles contain no workers earning more than $102,000, and about 0.1% of the families in the middle income quintile (quintile 3) contain such workers. Consequently, the average tax rates for the bottom three quintiles are largely unaffected by this policy option.

Table 2. Average Change in Annual Social Security Payroll Taxes

	Policy Option 1	Policy Option 2	Policy Option 3
All	$488	$0	$190
Quintile 1	$0	-$117	-$58
Quintile 2	$0	-$263	-$130
Quintile 3	$1	-$430	-$212
Quintile 4	$49	-$607	-$276
Quintile 5	$1,948	$754	$1,357
Top 10%	$3,460	$1,999	$2,737
Top 5%	$5,622	$3,908	$4,773
Top 1%	$10,877	$8,674	$9,786

Source: Author's analysis of the March 2009 Current Population Survey.
Note: The sample includes only families that contain at least one worker.

The average tax rate for the families in the top 40% of the income distribution, however, rises under policy option 1. The tax rate increases slightly for families in the fourth income quintile (from 10.97% to 11.03%) since only about 2% of these families contain a worker earning more than $102,000. The families in the top quintile, however, experience an 15% percent, or 1.3 percentage point, increase in their average tax rate. The average tax rate increases by 1.8 to 2.5 percentage points for families in the top 10% of the income distribution.

Policy option 2 raises the maximum taxable limit but reduces the tax rate so that total tax revenues remain unchanged. Since the policy is revenue neutral, the average tax rate for all families is the same as for current law (see the first row of Table 1). The average tax rate for most families, however, does change. The average rate falls for families in the bottom 80% of the income distribution (quintiles 1 to 4), and increases for families at the top. In general, workers earning less than $111,045 will pay less in payroll taxes than they do under current law; workers earning more than this will pay more in payroll taxes.

The final option, policy option 3, is a blend of the first two policy options. Half of the increased revenue from raising the maximum taxable limit is used for financing the Social Security program and the other half offsets a payroll tax rate reduction. As was the case with policy option 2, this policy option reduces the average tax rates for families in the bottom 80% of the income distribution and increases it for families in the top income quintile. For the richest 1% of families, this option raises the average tax rate by 2.3 percentage points, a 61% increase. The poorest 20% see their average tax rate fall by 0.4 percentage points, or by about 4%.

Table 2 provides an alternate view of the effects of the three policy options by reporting the simulated average dollar change in Social Security payroll taxes paid by families in different parts of the income distribution. The reported dollar amounts include the change in both the employee's and employer's portion of the payroll tax. It is important to keep in mind that a family may contain more than one worker.

The dollar changes are consistent with the changes in the average tax rates reported in Table 1. The first policy option increases the payroll tax for the average family by $488. This policy option does not affect families in the bottom two income quintiles and increases the tax payments for families in the middle quintile by only $1, on average. The average family in the richest income quintile would pay $1,948 more in taxes, and the richest 1% of families would pay, on average, $10,877 more in payroll taxes under this policy.

The second policy option is revenue neutral; consequently, the average tax change is zero. Families in the bottom four income quintiles would pay between $117 and $607 less in taxes, on average. Families in the top quintile would pay higher taxes (about $754, on average) and the richest 1% of families would pay $8,674 more.

The impact of policy option 3 on payroll tax payments follows the same patterns as policy option 2, but the amounts are larger. On average, families will pay $190 more in payroll taxes under this policy. However, families in the bottom 80% of the income distribution will pay lower taxes, on average. High-income families (the top quintile) pay $1,357 more in taxes, while the richest 1% pay about $9,800 more in payroll taxes.

Behavioral Effects of Tax Changes

It has been argued that the revenue increases from raising the payroll tax base would be significantly less than expected because of indirect behavioral changes by workers. Based on this interpretation, workers may respond to having more earnings subject to the payroll tax, which in effect is a reduction in earnings, by reducing their work effort (a labor supply effect) or shifting their income to forms that are not subject to the payroll tax (a taxable income effect). These behavioral effects would thus reduce taxable earnings, the proportion of family income subject to payroll taxes, and tax revenue.[15] As discussed below, however, recent research raises doubts concerning this position and suggests these behavioral effects would likely be negligible.

Relatively few families would be negatively affected by the three policy options examined. Of the families with at least one worker, about 10% contain a worker earning more than the maximum taxable limit (see Table 3). Families in the bottom two income quintiles contain no workers earning more than the maximum taxable limit ($102,000 in 2008). And few families in the next two quintiles contain high-earning workers—0.1% of the families in the middle quintile and about 2% of the fourth quintile. About 30% of the families in the richest income quintile contain workers earning more than the maximum taxable limit. The percentage is significantly higher for the richest 10% of families. Consequently, most of the 6% of families with high-earning workers are at the top of the income distribution—71% are in the richest 10% of U.S. families.

For the few families with high-earning workers, changing the payroll tax rate can affect labor supply in two possible ways. The first is the direct effect in which tax changes affect the wage received by the worker. Reducing wages could lead to a reduction in work effort (that is, labor supply). The empirical evidence indicates that men's labor supply is relatively inelastic (that is, changes in the wage have little effect on labor supply) with estimated elasticities close to zero.[16] In the past, women's labor force behavior differed significantly from that of men. This was especially true for married women. But recent research indicates a convergence in the labor force behavior of the sexes. A recent study suggests that over the past two decades, women's labor supply elasticities have fallen and converged with that of men.[17] One study, specifically examining the effect of the payroll tax on women's labor supply, concludes there is a work disincentive effect for women over 50.[18] Since about 3.5% of women over 50 earn more than the maximum taxable limit, few would potentially be affected by the three policy options analyzed. Furthermore, this study is based on labor force data from the 1970s—a time when women's labor supply was more responsive to wage changes.

The second effect is an indirect effect in which a change in the wage of one spouse affects the labor supply of the other spouse. Empirical studies, however, suggest married men are largely unresponsive to changes in their wives' wages with estimated elasticities close to zero.[19] While women's labor supply, however, is thought to be responsive to changes in their husband's wage, recent research suggests women's responsiveness has declined over the past two decades.[20]

Table 3. High-Earning Workers and Taxable Earnings by Quintile, 2008

	Percentage of Families with at Least One Worker Earning More than Maximum Taxable Limit	Taxable Earnings as a Percentage of Total Family Income
All	6.4%	77.9%
Quintile 1	0.0	83.8
Quintile 2	0.0	85.1
Quintile 3	0.1	87.4
Quintile 4	2.1	88.4
Quintile 5	29.9	68.8
Top 10%	49.1	60.0
Top 5%	72.2	49.0
Top 1%	98.5	30.1

Source: Author's analysis of the March 2009 Current Population Survey.
Note: The sample includes only families that contain at least one worker.

The cited studies suggest that raising the maximum taxable limit will have little effect on workers' labor supply. Relatively few workers earn enough to be affected by such a policy change (about 7% of all workers earn more than the maximum taxable limit). Additionally, men's labor supply appears largely unaffected by changes in their own wage and their spouse's wage. And women's labor supply behavior has increasingly become like that of men, and consequently they too appear largely unaffected by changes in their own wage and their spouse's wage.

While work effort or labor supply may not be affected by changes in the payroll tax, earnings subject to the payroll tax may be affected. In the aggregate, about three-quarters of U.S. families' income comes from taxable earnings (see the last column of Table 3). Of the rest, most comes from earnings above the maximum taxable limit, retirement income (Social Security and pension income), and investment returns (interest, dividends, and rental income). The proportion of family income from taxable earnings is over 80% for the bottom 80% of the income distribution. While the richest 20% of families derive about 69% of their income from taxable earnings. This proportion falls to under 50% for the richest 5% of families, and to about 30% for the richest 1%. Consequently, there may be some opportunities for workers with earnings more than the maximum taxable limit to shift their earnings to a nontaxable form of compensation.

The economics research before 2000 generally suggests taxable income is responsive to changes in marginal tax rates.[21] As marginal tax rates rise, the pre-2000 studies indicate taxpayers reduced their taxable income through tax avoidance strategies or tax evasion. They can do this by increasing deductions to reduce taxable income or by taking compensation in forms that are untaxed (such as stock options, which are untaxed until exercised) or subject to lower tax rates. A recent study, however, concludes that methodological problems lead to the estimated elasticities likely being overstated.[22]

More recent research suggests that the earlier results may have been due to the behavior of a few taxpayers in the extreme upper part of the income distribution.[23] Several recent studies estimate that taxable income is much less responsive to changes in tax rates and suggest that relatively large increases in tax rates could lead to relatively small decreases in taxable income.[24] In addition, one study found that tax rate changes have no effect on wages, one component of taxable income.[25] Raising the maximum taxable limit would increase the marginal tax rate on wages, but this recent empirical research suggests that workers' wage earnings would be largely unaffected.[26] This research also suggests that reducing the payroll tax rate (as in policy options 2 and 3) would not affect workers' behavior.

End Notes

[1] CBO, *Historical Effective Federal Tax Rates: 1979 to 2006*, April 2009. Social insurance payroll taxes include Social Security and Medicare payroll plus Unemployment Insurance payroll taxes.

[2] U.S. Congress, Joint Committee on Taxation, *General Explanation of the Revenue Act of 1978*, joint committee print, 96th Cong., 1st sess., Mar. 12, 1979 (Washington: GPO, 1979), p. 51.

[3] Covered earnings are earnings from employment covered by the Social Security and Medicare programs. Most workers in the United States are covered by the Social Security and Medicare programs. Some federal, state, and local workers, however, are not covered by these programs. The Health Care and Education Reconciliation Act of 2010 (P.L. 111-152) increased the Medicare payroll by 0.9 percentage points for high income taxpayers (to 3.8%).

[4] Most economists agree that workers ultimately bear the full burden of the payroll tax. Employers typically pass on their share of the payroll tax to employees through paying lower wages. See CBO, *Effective Federal Tax Rates, 1979- 1997*, October 2001.

[5] The maximum taxable limit is adjusted annually to keep pace with changes in average earnings. Covered earnings below the maximum taxable limit are referred to as taxable earnings.

[6] This projection is based on the Trustees' intermediate cost assumptions. Under the low cost assumptions, Social Security does not face long-term financial problems, and under the high cost assumptions, the Social Security trust funds will be depleted in 2031. See The Board of Trustees, *The 2009 Annual Report of the Board of Trustees of the Federal Old-Age and*

Survivors Insurance and Federal Disability Insurance Trust Funds, May 12, 2009 (Washington: GPO, 2009).

[7] Provisions in the 1977 amendments to the Social Security Act were designed to increase the percentage of covered earnings subject to the payroll tax to 90% by 1982.

[8] CBO, *Budget Options*, volume 2, August 2009, p. 234.

[9] Dalton Conley, "Turning the Tax Tables to Help the Poor," *New York Times*, Nov. 15, 2004, p. A21.

[10] Robert G. Valletta, *Computer Use and the U.S. Wage Distribution, 1984-2003*, Federal Reserve Bank of San Francisco Working Paper 2006-34, October 2006.

[11] The data source for the simulations is the Annual Social and Economic Supplement of the March 2009 Current Population Survey (CPS). For this survey, the Census Bureau collects survey information for over 200,000 people living in almost 100,000 households. The survey is representative of the civilian noninstitutionalized population in the United States. The March supplement includes detailed information on family and individual income for the previous year.

[12] Families are assigned to income quintiles based on equivalence-adjusted total family income (total family income divided by an equivalence scale). The equivalence scale is the one proposed by the National Research Council. See Constance F. Citro and Robert T. Michael, eds., *Measuring Poverty: A New Approach* (Washington, DC: National Academy Press, 1995).

[13] The average tax rate for high-income families may be artificially high because income components are top-coded (that is, cut-off at a particular amount) in the CPS by the Census Bureau to prevent identification of high-income individuals.

[14] The results are broadly consistent with an analysis by CBO. Any differences are due to differences in the unit of analysis (family versus household), income definition and data source. See CBO, *Historical Effective Federal Tax Rates: 1979 to 2006*, April 2009.

[15] D. Mark Wilson, *Removing Social Security's Tax Cap on Wages Would Do More Harm Than Good*, Heritage Foundation, Center for Data Analysis Report #01-07, Oct. 17, 2001.

[16] Mark R. Killingsworth, *Labor Supply* (New York: Cambridge University Press, 1983), and Richard Blundell and Thomas MaCurdy, "Labor Supply: A Review of Alternative Approaches," in Orley Ashenfelter and David Card, eds., *Handbook of Labor Economics* (Amsterdam: Elsevier, 1999), pp. 1559-1695.

[17] Francine D. Blau and Lawrence M. Kahn, "Changes in the Labor Supply Behavior of Married Women: 1980-2000," *Journal of Labor Economics*, vol. 25, no. 3 (July 2007), pp. 393-438.

[18] Therese A. McCarty, "The Effect of Social Security on Married Women's Labor Force Participation," *National Tax Journal*, vol. 43, no. 1 (March 1990), pp. 95-110.

[19] Paul J. Devereux, "Changes in Relative Wages and Family Labor Supply," *Journal of Human Resources*, vol. 39 (Summer 2004), pp. 696-722, and Francine D. Blau and Lawrence M. Kahn, *Changes in the Labor Supply Behavior of Married Women: 1980-2000*, National Bureau of Economic Research, Working Paper no. 11230, March 2005.

[20] Francine D. Blau and Lawrence M. Kahn, *Changes in the Labor Supply Behavior of Married Women: 1980-2000*, National Bureau of Economic Research, Working Paper no. 11230, March 2005.

[21] Martin Feldstein, "The Effect of Marginal Tax Rates on Taxable Income: A Panel Study of the 1986 Tax Reform Act," *Journal of Political Economy*, vol. 103, no. 3 (1995), pp. 551-572; and Gerald Auten and Robert Carroll, "The Effect of Income Taxes on Household Behavior," *Review of Economics and Statistics*, vol. 81, no. 3 (1999), pp. 681- 693.

[22] CRS Report RL33672, *Revenue Feedback from the 2001-2004 Tax Cuts*, by Jane G. Gravelle.

[23] Robert A. Moffitt and Mark O. Wilhelm, "Taxation and the Labor Supply Decisions of the Affluent," in Joel B. Slemrod, ed., *Does Atlas Shrug? The Economic*

Consequences of Taxing the Rich (Cambridge, MA: Harvard University Press, 2002).

[24] Jon Gruber and Emmanuel Saez, "The Elasticity of Taxable Income: Evidence and Implications," *Journal of Public Economics*, vol. 84 (2002), pp. 1-32; and Emmanuel Saez, "The Effect of Marginal Tax Rates on Income: A Panel Study of 'Bracket Creep,'" *Journal of Public Economics*, vol. 87 (2003), pp. 1231-1258.

[25] Emmanuel Saez, "The Effect of Marginal Tax Rates on Income: A Panel Study of 'Bracket Creep,'" *Journal of Public Economics*, vol. 87 (2003), pp. 1231-1258.

[26] Workers with earnings above the higher maximum taxable limit of $213,900 would not face an increase in the marginal tax rate after the change—their marginal tax rate would remain at zero.

In: Social Security: Background, Issues and... ISBN: 978-1-61761-469-9
Editors: Jacob T. Álvarez

Chapter 7

SOCIAL SECURITY: CALCULATION AND HISTORY OF TAXING BENEFITS

Christine Scott and Janemarie Mulvey

SUMMARY

Social Security provides monthly benefits to qualified retirees, disabled workers, and their spouses and dependents. Until 1984, Social Security benefits were exempt from the federal income tax. In 1983, Congress approved recommendations from the National Commission on Social Security Reform (also known as the Greenspan Commission) to tax Social Security benefits above a specified income threshold. Specifically, beginning in 1984, up to 50% of Social Security and Railroad Retirement Board (RRB) Tier 1 benefits are taxable for individuals whose provisional income exceeds $25,000. The threshold is $32,000 for married couples. Provisional income is defined as the total income from all sources recognized for tax purposes plus certain otherwise tax-exempt income, including half of Social Security and RRB Tier 1 benefits. The proceeds from taxing Social Security and Railroad Retirement Tier I benefits at the 50% rate are credited to the Old-Age and Survivors Insurance (OASI) trust fund, the Disability Insurance (DI) trust fund, and the Railroad Retirement system respectively, based on the source of the benefit taxed.

In 1993, Congress passed a second income threshold for the calculation of taxable Social Security and RRB Tier I benefits. This second threshold (often referred to as Tier 2) taxes up to 85% of benefits for individuals whose provisional income exceeds $34,000 and for married couples whose provisional income exceeds $44,000. The tax proceeds from the second tier goes to the Medicare Hospital Insurance (HI) Trust Fund.

Income from taxation of benefits to the Social Security trust funds totaled $16.9 billion in 2008, or 2.1% of its total income. For Medicare, income from taxation of benefits totaled $11.7 billion in 2008, or 5.1% of total HI trust fund income. Because the income thresholds to determine the taxation of Social Security benefits are not indexed for inflation or wage growth, the share of beneficiaries affected by these thresholds is expected to increase over time. According to the Congressional Budget Office (CBO), 39% of (or 16.9 million) Social Security beneficiaries were affected by the income taxation of Social Security benefits in 2005.

In the 111th Congress, legislation has been introduced that would impact the taxation of Social Security benefits by indexing the income thresholds, repealing the taxation of benefits at the 85% level, and repealing all taxation of Social Security benefits.

The Social Security system provides monthly benefits to qualified retirees, disabled workers, and their spouses and dependents. Until 1984, Social Security benefits were exempt from the federal income tax. Then in 1984, Congress enacted legislation to begin to tax Social Security benefits with a formula for determining taxable benefits that gradually increased as a person's income rose above a specified income threshold. In 1993, a second income threshold was added that increased the share of benefits that are taxable. These two thresholds are often referred to as Tier 1 and Tier 2.

Calculation of Taxable Social Security Benefits

In general, the Social Security and Tier I Railroad Retirement[1] benefits of most recipients are not subject to the income tax. However, up to 85% of Social Security and Tier I Railroad Retirement benefits can be included in taxable income for recipients whose "provisional income" exceeds either of two statutory thresholds (based on filing status).[2]

"Provisional income" is total income,[3] *plus* certain otherwise tax-exempt income (tax-exempt interest), *plus* the addition (or adding back) of certain income specifically excluded from federal income taxation (interest on certain U.S. savings bonds,[4] employer-provided adoption benefits, foreign earned income or foreign housing, and income earned in Puerto Rico or American Samoa by bona fide residents), and *plus* one-half (5 0%) of Social Security and Tier I Railroad Retirement benefits.

The thresholds below which no Social Security or Tier I benefits are taxable are $25,000 for taxpayers filing as single, head of household, or qualifying widow(er) and $32,000 for taxpayers filing a joint return. A taxpayer who is married filing separately who has lived apart from his or her spouse all tax year has a threshold amount of $25,000. A taxpayer who is married filing separately who lived with his or her spouse at any point during the tax year, has a threshold amount of $0.

If provisional income is between the first tier thresholds of $25,000 (single) or $32,000 (married couple) and the second tier thresholds of $34,000 (single) or $44,000 (married couple), the amount of Social Security and Tier I benefits subject to tax is the lesser of (1) one-half (50%) of Social Security and Tier I benefits; or (2) one-half (50%) of provisional income in excess of the first threshold.

If income is above the second tier threshold, the amount of Social Security and Tier I Railroad Retirement benefits subject to tax is the lesser of (1) 85% of Social Security and Tier I benefits; or (2) 85% of provisional income above the second threshold, plus the smaller of (a) $4,500 (single) or $6,000 (married couple);[5] or (b) one-half (50%) of Social Security and Tier I benefits.

Because the threshold for a married taxpayer filing separately who has lived with his or her spouse at any time during the tax year is $0, the taxable benefits in such a case are the lesser of 85% of Social Security and Tier I benefits or 85% of provisional income. None of the thresholds are indexed for inflation or wage growth. Table 1 summarizes the thresholds and calculation of taxable Social Security and Tier I Railroad Retirement benefits.

The following two examples in Table 2 illustrate how taxable Security benefits may be calculated for a single retiree in tax year 2008. The retiree is at least 62 years of age, and receives $12,948 in annual Social Security benefits—the average in December 2007 for a retiree.[6] The examples include other (non-Social Security) income of $22,000 or $32,000.

Table 1. Calculation of Taxable Social Security and Tier I Railroad Retirement Benefits

Provisional Income (*)	Calculation of Taxable Social Security and Tier I Railroad Retirement Benefits
Single Taxpayer	
Less than $25,000	No taxable Social Security or Tier I Railroad Retirement benefits
$25,000 less than $34,000	Lesser of (1) 50% of Social Security and Tier I benefits; or (2) 50% of provisional income above $25,000
More than $34,000	Lesser of (1) 85% of Social Security and Tier I benefits; or (2) 85% of provisional income above $34,000 plus lesser of (A) $4,500; or (B) 50% of Social Security and Tier I benefits
Married Taxpayer	
Less than $32,000	No taxable Social Security or Tier I Railroad Retirement benefits
$32,000 less than $44,000	Lesser of (1) 50% of Social Security benefits; or (2) 50% of provisional income above $32,000
More than $44,000	Lesser of (1) 85% of Social Security benefits; or (2) 85% of provisional income above $44,000 plus lesser of (A) $6,000; or (B) 50% of Social Security and Tier I benefits

Source: Table prepared by the Congressional Research Service (CRS).

Note: Provisional income is total income plus certain income exclusions plus one-half (50%) of Social Security benefits.

Table 2. Example of Calculation of Social Security Benefits for Average Social Security Recipient and Different Assumptions about Other Income

Step 1: Calculate Provisional Income	John	Mary
Other income	$22,000	$32,000
+ 50% of Social Security (assume Social Security benefits are $12,948)	$6,474	$6,474
=Provisional income	$28,474	$38,474

Table 2. (Continued)

Step 2: Compare Provisional Income to 1st Tier Threshold		
First tier threshold	$25,000	$25,000
Calculate Excess over First Tier Threshold Lesser of • Provisional income minus first tier threshold or		
• Difference between first and second tier thresholds [$9,000]	$3,474	$9,000
First tier taxable benefits Equals Lesser of • 50% of Social Security or tier I benefits or		
• 50% of excess over first tier	$1,737	$4,500
Step 3: Compare Prov. Income To 2nd Tier Threshold		
Second tier threshold	*$34,000*	*$34,000*
Calculate Excess over second tier		
• Provisional income minus second tier threshold	$0	$4,474
Second tier taxable benefits 85% of excess	$0	$3,803
Step 4: Calculate Total Taxable Social Security Benefits		
If provisional income is less than $34,000, total taxable benefits equal first tier taxable benefits.		
If provisional income is greater than $34,000, total taxable benefits equal the lesser of • 85% of Social Security benefits (=$11,006) or		
• First tier taxable benefits plus second tier taxable benefits	$1,737	$8,303

Source: Table prepared by the Congressional Research Service (CRS).

Figure 1 shows taxable Social Security benefits for a single retiree with Social Security benefits of $12,948 as non-Social Security income (and provisional income) increases. Shown on the figure is the point at which taxable benefits are calculated using the Tier 2 formula in which the comparisons in the formula use a ratio of 85% (rather than the 50% ratio for Tier 1). At this point, each additional dollar of non-Social Security income results in a larger increase in taxable Social Security benefits (because of the ratio change from 50% to 85% in the calculations). In Figure 1, the taxable Social Security benefits reach a maximum of 85% of Social Security benefits (illustrated by a flattening of the line) when non-Social Security income equals $34,000 in this example.

The calculation of taxable Social Security benefits depends on the level of benefits, the tax filing status, and non-Social Security income. Holding non-Social Security income constant, as benefits increase, taxable Social Security benefits will increase. For the same levels of non-Social Security income and Social Security benefits, a married couple will have lower taxable Social Security benefits than a single retiree. Consequently, Figure 1 does not reflect other levels of benefits, or the impact of taxation on a married couple filing a joint tax return.

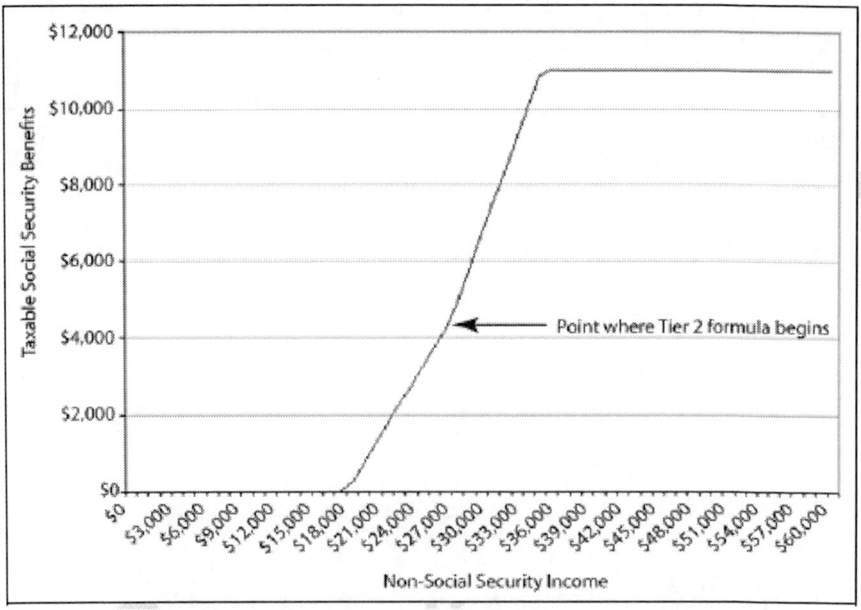

Source: Figure prepared by the Congressional Research Service (CRS).

Figure 1 . Taxable Social Security Benefits as Non-Social Security (and Provisional) Income Increases for a Single Retiree with $12,948 in Annual Social Security Benefits,TaxYear 2008

Table 3. State Income Taxation of Social Security Benefits, Tax Year 2008

States taxing all or part of the federal taxable Social Security benefits	Colorado, Connecticut, Iowa,a Kansas, Minnesota, Missouri,a Montana, Nebraska, New Mexico, North Dakota, Rhode Island, Utah, Vermont, West Virginia
States excluding Social Security benefits from state personal income taxes	Alabama, Arizona, Arkansas, California, Delaware, District of Columbia, Georgia, Hawaii, Idaho, Indiana, Illinois, Kentucky, Louisiana, Maine, Maryland, Massachusetts, Michigan, Mississippi, New Jersey, New York, North Carolina, Ohio, Oklahoma, Oregon, Pennsylvania, South Carolina, Virginia and Wisconsin
States without a state personal income tax	Alaska, Florida, Nevada, New Hampshire, South Dakota, Tennessee, Texas, Washington, Wyoming

Source: Minnesota House of Representatives, House Research; available at http://www.house.leg.state.mn.us/ hrd/issinfo/sstaxes.htm.

a. Iowa will fully exempt benefits in 2014, and Missouri will fully exempt benefits beginning in tax year 2012.

Special Considerations

There are special considerations in which the application of the taxation of benefits formula may vary. These include lump sum distributions, repayments, coordination of workers compensation, treatment of non-residential aliens, and withholding from wages. Each of these issues is discussed in more detail in the Appendix to this chapter.

State Taxation

Although the Railroad Retirement Act prohibits states from taxing railroad retirement benefits (including any federally taxable Tier I benefits), states may tax Social Security benefits. In general, state personal income taxes follow federal taxes. That is, many states use as a beginning point for the state income tax calculations either federal adjusted gross income, federal taxable income, or federal taxes paid. All of these beginning points include the federally taxed portion of Social Security benefits. States with these beginning points for state taxation must then make an adjustment, or subtraction from income (or taxes), for railroad retirement benefits. A state may also make an adjustment for all or part or the federally taxed Social Security benefits. Some states do not begin the calculation of state income taxes with these federal tax values, but instead begin with a calculation based on income by source. The state may then include part or all of Social Security benefits[7] in the state calculation of income.

In tax year 2008, 28 of the 41 states (and the District of Columbia) with a personal income tax, fully excluded Social Security benefits from the state personal income tax. Fourteen states tax all, or part, of Social Security benefits. Nine states do not have an income tax or have a tax limited to specific kinds of unearned income. Table 3 identifies what states fall into each of these categories for tax year 2008.

Impact of Taxing Social Security Benefits

Because the income thresholds to determine the taxation of Social Security benefits are not indexed for inflation or wage growth, the share of beneficiaries affected by these thresholds is increasing over time.

Table 4. Number and Percentage of Beneficiaries with Taxable Social Security Benefits by Income Class Under 2005

Level of Income	Number of Social Security Beneficiaries (in thousands)	Number of Beneficiaries Affected by Taxation (in thousands)	Percentage of Beneficiaries Affected by Taxation
Less than$10,000	5,957	0	0.0%
$10,000 - $15,000	5,201	4	0.1%
$15,000 - $20,000	3,688	12	0.3%
$20,000 - $25,000	3,347	11	0.3%
$25,000 - $30,000	2,917	76	2.6%
$30,000 - $40,000	5,260	1,478	28.1%
$40,000 - $50,000	4,497	3,168	70.4%
$50,000 - $100,000	8,931	8,578	96.0%
Over $100,000	3,632	3,607	99.3%
Total	43,429	16,934	39.0%

Source: Congressional Budget Office simulations based on data from the Statistics of Income and supplemented by data from the Current Population Survey.

Notes: Income is defined as AGI plus statutory adjustments, tax-exempt interest, and nontaxable Social Security benefits. Number of Social Security beneficiaries includes beneficiaries under and over age 65.

According to the Congressional Budget Office (CBO), 39% of (or 16.9 million) Social Security beneficiaries were affected by the income taxation of Social Security benefits in 2005. This compares to 32% of Social Security beneficiaries affected by taxation of benefit in 2000 and 26% in 1998.[8]

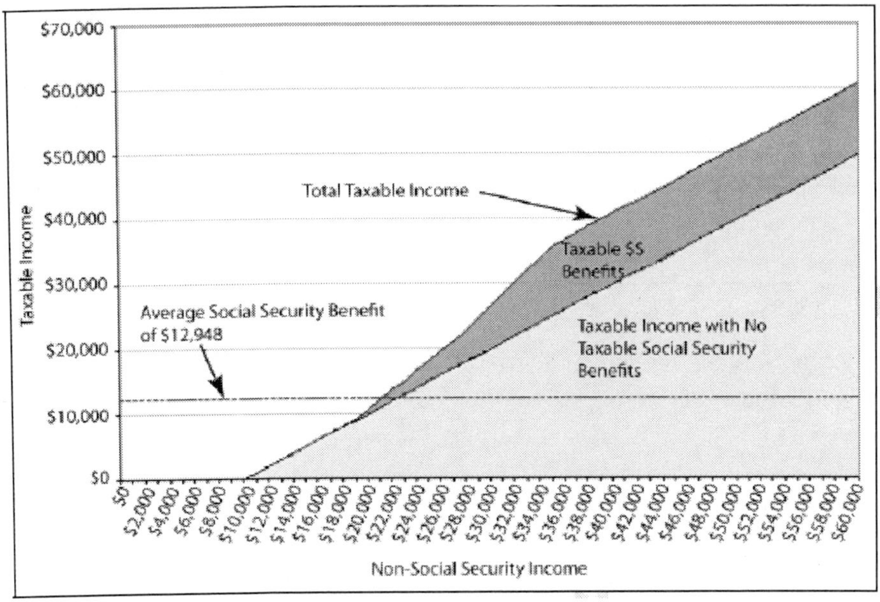

Source: Figure prepared by congressional Research Service (CRS).

Figure 2. Taxable Income for an Average Single Retiree Tax Year 2008

Table 4 shows the CBO estimates of the number of Social Security beneficiaries, the number of beneficiaries affected by the taxation of Social Security benefits, and the percent of beneficiaries affected by taxation by level of income (cash income for the tax unit plus capital gains realizations). As shown in Table 4, the percentage of Social Security beneficiaries affected increases with the income level, with more than 90% of beneficiaries with an income of $40,000 or more affected by the taxation of Social Security benefits

As previously noted, because of the thresholds not all Social Security benefits are taxable. Figure 2 shows how Social Security benefits impact taxable income for a given level of Social Security benefits ($12, 948) for a single retiree in tax year 2008.[9] As non-Social Security income increases, more of Social Security benefits become taxable. This leads to an increase in overall taxable income. Because the taxation of Social Security benefits is capped at 85% in the second tier, the darkly shaded area in Figure 2 shows that the amount of Social Security benefits that are taxed remains constant as non-Social Security income increases beyond the second threshold.

Figure 3 shows how different levels of Social Security benefits affect taxable income for a single retiree with either $20,000 or $30,000 in non-Social Security income.[10] In Figure 3, the Social Security benefits increase until they reach the annual maximum benefits for a person receiving benefits at full retirement age (65 years and 10 months) in 2008—$26,220.

Table 5 shows the impact of rising income on the share of benefits that are taxed for the U.S. taxpayers in 2005. Level of income includes cash income plus capital gains realizations. As shown in Table 5, as income increases, taxes as a percent of Social Security benefits rises.

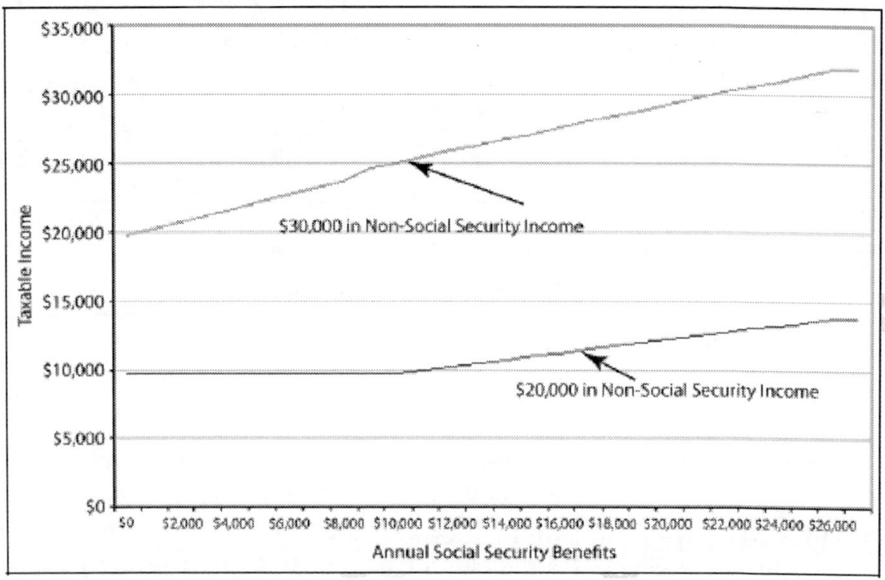

Source: Figure prepared by the Congressional Research Service (CRS). Assumes Social Security benefits increase to $26,220—the maximum benefit in 2008 for a person retiring in 2008 at full retirement age (65 years and 10 months of age).

Figure 3. Taxable Income for a Single Retiree with $20,000 or $30,000 in Non-Social Security Income as Annual Social Security Benefits Increase, Tax Year 2008

Table 5. Social Security Benefits and Taxes on Social Security Benefits by Income Class Under 2005 Law

Level of Income	Social Security Benefits (in millions)	Taxes on Social Security Benefits (in millions)	Taxes as a Percent of Benefits
Less than $10,000	$40,403	$0	0.0%
$10,000 - $15,000	$53,769	$1	0.0%
$15,000 - $20,000	$40,480	$4	0.0%
$20,000 - $25,000	$36,927	$9	0.0%
$25,000 - $30,000	$33,009	$17	0.1%
$30,000 - $40,000	$59,893	$390	0.7%
$40,000 - $50,000	$51,717	$1,412	2.7%
$50,000 - $100,000	$110,421	$11,508	10.4%
Over $100,000	$49,378	$10,767	21.8%
Total	$475,997	$24,107	5.1%

Source: Congressional Budget Office simulations based on data from the Statistics of Income and supplemented by data from the Current Population Survey.

Notes: Income is defined as AGI plus statutory adjustments, tax-exempt interest, and nontaxable Social Security benefits. Number of Social Security beneficiaries includes beneficiaries under and over age 65.

Impact on the Trust Funds

The proceeds from taxing Social Security and Tier I benefits at the 50% rate are credited to the Old-Age and Survivors Insurance (OASI) trust fund, the Disability Insurance (DI) trust fund and the Railroad Retirement system respectively, on the basis of the source of the benefits taxed. Proceeds from taxing Social Security benefits and Tier I benefits at the 85% rate are credited to the Hospital Insurance trust fund (HI) of Medicare. In 2008, the Trustees Report reported income to OASDI of $16.9 billion from the taxation of benefits, or 2.1% of the combined income for both funds.[11] Income from the taxation of benefits in the HI fund were $11.7 billion, or 5.1% of total HI fund income. [12] Income taxes transferred to support railroad retirement programs were comparatively smaller, $359 million, in 2008.[13]

HISTORY OF TAXING SOCIAL SECURITY BENEFITS

Until 1984, Social Security benefits were exempt from the federal income tax. The exclusion was based on rulings made in 1938 and 1941 by the Department of the Treasury, Bureau of Internal Revenue (the predecessor of the Internal Revenue Service). The 1941 Bureau ruling on OASDI payments viewed benefits as being for general welfare and reasoned that subjecting the payments to income taxation would be contrary to the purposes of Social Security.[14]

Under these rules, the treatment of Social Security benefits was similar to that of certain types of government transfer payments (such as Aid to Families with Dependent Children, Supplemental Security Income, and black lung benefits). This was in sharp contrast to then-current rules for retirement benefits under private pension plans, the Federal Civil Service Retirement System (CSRS), and other government pension systems. Benefits from these other pension plans were fully taxable, except for the portion of total lifetime benefits (using projected life expectancy) attributable to the employee's own contributions to the system (and on which he or she had already paid income tax).

Currently (and as in 1941), under Social Security the worker's contribution to the system is his or her share (one-half (50%)) of the payroll tax, officially known as the Federal Insurance Contributions Act (FICA) tax. The amount the worker pays into the Social Security system in FICA taxes is not subtracted to determine income subject to the federal income tax, and is therefore taxed. The employer's contributions to the system are not considered part of the employee's gross income, and are deductible from the employer's business income as a business expense. Consequently, neither the employee or the employer pays taxes on the employer's contribution.

The 1979 Advisory Council on Social Security concluded that the 1941 ruling was wrong and that the tax treatment of private pensions was a more appropriate model for tax treatment of Social Security benefits.[15] The council estimated that the most anyone who entered the workforce in 1979 would pay in payroll taxes during his or her lifetime would equal 17% of the Social Security benefits he or she would ultimately receive. (This was the most any individual would pay; in the aggregate, workers would make payroll tax payments amounting to substantially less than 17% of their ultimate benefits.) Because of the administrative difficulties involved in determining the taxable amount of each individual benefit, the council recommended instead that half of everyone's benefit be taxed. They justified this ratio as a matter of "rough justice" and noted that it coincided with the portion of the tax (the employer's share) on which income taxes had not been paid. This position to tax Social Security benefits was in contrast to the position of the National Commission on Social Security, established by Congress in the Social Security Amendments of 1977 (P.L. 95-216). The commission did not, in its 1981 final report, include a recommendation to tax Social Security benefits.

The National Commission on Social Security Reform (often referred to as the "Greenspan Commission"), appointed by President Reagan in 1981, recommended in its 1983 report[16] that, beginning in 1984, one-half (50%) of Social Security cash benefits and Tier I benefits payable under the Railroad Retirement Act be taxable for individuals whose adjusted gross income, excluding Social Security cash benefits, exceeded certain thresholds—$20,000 for a single taxpayer, and $25,000 for a married couple, with the proceeds of such taxation credited to the Social Security trust funds. The commission did not include any provisions for indexing the threshold amounts. The commission estimated that 10% of OASDI recipients would be subject to taxation of benefits. The commission acknowledged that the proposal had a "notch" problem, in that the extra dollar of income that would put one over the threshold would have had the effect of subjecting fully one-half (50%) of Social Security benefits to taxation, but trusted that it would be rectified during the legislative process.

In enacting the 1983 Social Security Amendments (P.L. 98-21), Congress adopted the commission's recommendation to tax Social Security benefits, but with a formula for determining taxable benefits that gradually increased as a person's income rose above the thresholds, up to a maximum of one-half (50%) of benefits. The formula calculated taxable benefits as the lesser of one-half (5 0%) of benefits or one-half (5 0%) of the excess of the taxpayer's provisional income over thresholds of $25,000 (single) and $32,000 (married couple). Provisional income was defined as total income plus certain tax-exempt income (tax-exempt interest) plus certain income exclusions plus one-half (5 0%) of Social Security benefits. At the same time, the tax credit for the elderly and disabled was expanded to provide additional tax relief for lower income elderly taxpayers.[17]

In 1993, the Social Security Administration's Office of the Actuary estimated that, if pension tax rules were applied to Social Security, the ratio of total employee Social Security payroll taxes to expected benefits for current recipients (in 1993) would be approximately 4% or 5%. The actuarial estimates were that for workers just entering the workforce,[18] the ratio would be, on average, about 7%. Because Social Security benefits replaced a higher proportion of earnings of workers who were lower paid and had dependents, and because women had longer life expectancies, the workers with the highest ratio of taxes to benefits would be single, highly paid males. The estimated ratio for these workers (highly paid males)entering the workforce in 1993 was 15%.

Applying the tax rules for private and public pensions presents practical administrative problems. Determining the proper exclusion would be complex for several reasons, including calculating the ratio of contributions to benefits for each individual worker's account when, unlike private pensions, several people may receive benefits on the basis of the same worker's account.

President Clinton proposed (as part of his FY1 994 budget proposal) that the portion of Social Security benefits subject to taxation be increased from 50% to 85%, effective in tax year 1994. As under then-current law, only Social Security recipients whose provisional income exceeded the thresholds of $25,000 (single) and $32,000 (married couple) were to pay taxes on their benefits. Also as under then-current law, the first step was to add one-half (50%), not 85%, of benefits to total income. Because the thresholds and definition of provisional income did not change, the measure would only affect recipients already paying taxes on benefits. However, the ratio used to compute the amount of taxable benefits was increased from 50% to 85%. Taxing no more than 85% of Social Security benefits (the portion not based on contributions by a recipient, including highly paid males) would ensure that no one would have a higher percentage of Social Security benefits subject to tax than if the tax treatment of private and civil service pensions were actually applied.

The proceeds from the increase (from 50% to 85%) were slated to be credited to the Medicare Hospital Insurance program, which had a less favorable financial outlook than Social Security at that time. Doing so also avoided possible procedural obstacles (budget points of order that can be raised regarding changes to the Social Security program in the budget reconciliation process). This measure was included in the 1993 Omnibus Budget Reconciliation Act (OBRA), which passed the House on May 27, 1993.

The Senate version of the bill included a provision to tax Social Security benefits up to 85% but imposed it only after provisional income exceeded new thresholds of $32,000 (single) and $40,000 (married couple). When the House and Senate versions of the budget package were negotiated in conference, the conference agreement adopted the Senate version of the taxation of Social Security benefits provision and raised the thresholds to $34,000 (single) and

$44,000 (married couple). President Clinton signed the measure into law (as part of P.L. 103-66) on August 10, 1993.

Appendix. Special Considerations under Taxation of Benefits

Lump Sum Distributions

A Social Security beneficiary may receive a lump sum distribution of benefits for one or more prior years.[19] In this situation, a beneficiary has the option of choosing between two methods for calculating the taxable portion of the benefits for prior years: (1) the taxpayer may include all of the benefits for prior years in calculating the taxable benefits for the current year; or (2) the taxpayer may re-calculate the prior year taxable benefits using prior year income and take the difference between the recalculated taxable benefits and the taxable benefits reported in each prior year. In computing the taxable portion of benefits in prior years, the provisional income for the prior years is adjusted gross income plus tax exempt interest plus the excluded income (as detailed earlier) plus the addition (or add-back) of the adjustment for student loan interest, plus one-half (50%) of Social Security benefits.

Repayments

Sometimes a Social Security beneficiary must repay a prior overpayment of benefits. In this case, the calculation of taxable Social Security benefits is based on the net benefits—gross benefits less the repayment. Married taxpayers filing a joint tax return would use the total of the net Social Security benefits for the tax year received by each party (taxpayer plus spouse). If however, the repayment results in negative net Social Security benefits, there are two consequences for taxes: (1) there are no taxable Social Security benefits; and (2) the taxpayer may take a miscellaneous deduction[20] as part of itemized deductions, or a credit for the negative net Social Security benefits. If the negative net Social Security benefits are less than $3,000, the taxpayer must include negative net Social Security benefits in miscellaneous deductions for computing itemized deductions. If the negative net Social Security benefits are greater than $3,000, the taxpayer must compute the current year tax liability two ways: (1) using the negative balance as a miscellaneous deduction for computing itemized deductions; and (2) re-computing the taxes (without the overpayment income) for the prior years in which an overpayment was received and subtracting these amounts from the prior year taxes paid, and then subtracting this result (the sum of the differences in prior year taxes) from the current year tax liability. If the tax liability computed using the negative balance as a miscellaneous deduction is lower, the taxpayer claims the deduction. If the tax liability from re-computing prior years taxes is lower, the taxpayer claims a tax credit equal to the sum of the prior year tax differences.

Coordination of Workers Compensation

Under current law, an individual's Social Security benefits (until the full retirement age), may be reduced by a portion of the Workers Compensation payments (payments from some other public disability program) received by the individual. Any reduction in Social Security benefits due to the receipt of Workers Compensation is considered to be a Social Security benefit and is used in determining the amount of Social Security benefits subject to taxation.

Treatment of Nonresident Aliens

Citizenship is not required for receipt of Social Security benefits. Aliens may receive benefits provided they have engaged in covered employment and otherwise meet eligibility requirements. In general, 85% of the Social Security benefits for nonresident aliens is subject to income tax (i.e., none of the thresholds apply). However, there are a number of exceptions to this general rule on the basis of tax treaties such that nonresident aliens or U.S. citizens living abroad may not have U.S. Social Security benefits subject to U.S. income taxes.[21]

Withholding

In general, withholding for a wage earner is based on the estimated income taxes for a full year of earnings at the periodic (weekly, bi-weekly, monthly, etc.) rate. Taxable Social Security benefits, and the associated taxes, are based on the amount of non-Social Security income earned by a recipient during the tax year. The Social Security Administration, without knowledge about the amount of other income received by a beneficiary, is unable to properly determine the amount of taxes that should be withheld from Social Security benefits. Like other non-wage earners, Social Security recipients can make quarterly estimated income tax payments. The Uruguay Round Agreements Act (P.L. 103-465) amended the Internal Revenue Code (IRC) to allow individuals to request that monies be withheld from certain federal payments to satisfy their income tax liability (this is commonly referred to as voluntary tax withholding). An amendment to Section 207 of the Social Security Act allowed this voluntary tax withholding from Social Security benefits.[22] Voluntary tax withholding became effective with payments issued in February 1999.

The Economic Growth and Tax Relief Reconciliation Act of 2001 (P.L. 107-16) permitted voluntary withholding from Social Security benefits at rates of 7%, and equal to the bottom three tax bracket tax rates (currently 10%, 15%, and 25%). This P.L. 107-16 change will expire on December 31, 2010.

Aliens residing outside the United States are subject to different tax withholding rules. Section 871 of the Internal Revenue Code imposes an arbitrary rate of tax withholding (3 0%) on almost all of the U.S. income of nonresident aliens, unless a lower rate is fixed by treaty. Thus, 30% of 85% (or 25.5%) of a nonresident alien's Social Security benefits may be withheld for federal income taxes.

End Notes

[1] Tier I railroad retirement benefits are paid to a qualified railroad retiree who has met the quarterly work requirements for Social Security benefit eligibility. The retiree receives Social Security benefits based on the work history that qualified the retiree for Social Security benefits, and Tier I benefits based on both the Social Security and railroad work histories. The actual Social Security benefits received are subtracted from this calculation of Tier I benefits to get actual Tier I benefits.

[2] For additional information on calculating taxable Social Security benefits, see U.S. Department of the Treasury, Internal Revenue Service, "Social Security and Equivalent Railroad Retirement Benefits," *Publication 915*, 2006, available online at http://www.irs.gov/pub/irs-pdf/p915.pdf.

[3] Total income is the total of income from all sources recognized for tax purposes. See *Publication 915* for details on the sources of income included in computing provisional income.

[4] Interest on qualified U.S. savings bonds used to pay certain educational expenses is exempt from federal income taxation.

[5] The $4,500 (single) and $6,000 (married couple) amounts are the maximum taxes for the Tier I calculation, and are equivalent to one-half (50%) of the difference between the first and second tier thresholds.

[6] The average monthly OASI payment for a retiree in December 2007 was $1,079. This would be an annual payment amount of $12,948. Information on current monthly benefit payments is available by accessing beneficiary databases at http://www.ssa.gov/ OACT/ ProgData/icp.html.

[7] States that chose to tax Social Security benefits, generally tax up to the federally taxed amount.

[8] CBO estimates are reported in the Green Book, Committee on Ways and Means, U.S. House of Representatives (1998, 2000 and 2008 editions). Changes from year to year may also reflect changes to CBO's methodology and data sources over time.

[9] All tax calculations for this chapter are estimated by CRS. The taxpayer is assumed to have used the standard deduction, including the additional amount for the elderly and disabled.

[10] Ibid.

[11] Social Security Administration, *2009 Annual Report of the Board of Trustees of the Federal Old-Age and Survivors Insurance and Disability Insurance Trust Funds*, May 12, 2009, available at http://www.ssa.gov/OACT/TR/TR09/ tr09.pdf.

[12] Center for Medicare and Medicaid Services, *2009 Annual Report of the Board of Trustees of the Federal Hospital Insurance Trust and Federal Supplementary Medical Insurance Trust Funds*, May 12, 2009, available at http://www.cms.hhs.gov/ ReportsTrustFunds /downloads/tr2009.pdf.

[13] Railroad Retirement Board, 2008 Annual Report, available at http://www.rrb. gov/pdf/opa/annualrprt/ *annualreport*.pdf.

[14] U.S. Congress, Senate Committee on Finance, *Tax Free Status of Social Security Benefits, Report to Accompany S.Res. 87*, Comm. Rep. No. 97-135, June 15, 1981.

[15] U.S. Congress, Select Committee on Aging, *Hearings Before the Committee on Retirement Income And Employment, Oversight on Recommendations of the 1979 Social Security Advisory Council, Statement of Henry Aaron, Chairman of the Advisory Council on Social Security*, Comm. Pub. No. 96-230, March 11 and 13, 1980, p. 13.

[16] Social Security Administration, *Report of the National Commission on Social Security Reform*, January 1983, pp. 2- 10 through 2-11, available at*http://www.ssa.gov/history /reports/gspan.html.*

[17] The credit was originally created to provide a benefit to retirees that had taxable retirement income rather than nontaxable Social Security benefits.

[18] The average for all workers entering the work force is for all workers born in 1970 entering the workforce. The estimate for single males assumed the worker entering the work force in 1993 was 22 years old with steady income until retirement at either age 62 or the normal retirement age.

[19] This is not the lump-sum death benefit which is not subject to the federal income tax. An individual originally denied benefits, but approved on appeal, may receive a lump sum amount for the period when benefits were denied (which may be prior years).

[20] Miscellaneous itemized deductions are subject to a 2% floor. That is, they are included in itemized deductions to the extent they exceed 2% of adjusted gross income.

[21] Internal Revenue Service, *Publication 915* provides a lists of the countries whose citizens (as nonresident aliens) are exempt from U.S. income taxes of Social Security benefits, and countries where residing U.S. citizens are exempt.

[22] Because they are not subject to the federal income tax, Supplemental Security Income payments, Black Lung payments, Medicare premium refunds, Lump Sum Death Payments, returned check re-issuances, and benefits due before January 1984, are not subject to voluntary tax withholding.

In: Social Security: Background, Issues and... ISBN: 978-1-61761-469-9
Editors: Jacob T. Álvarez

Chapter 8

THE IMPACT OF MEDICARE PREMIUMS ON SOCIAL SECURITY BENEFICIARIES

Alison M. Shelton

SUMMARY

Most Social Security beneficiaries pay Medicare premiums. Beneficiaries who participate in Medicare Part B (Supplementary Medical Insurance) or Part D (prescription drugs) must pay monthly premiums, unless they qualify for low-income assistance. Part B participants who also receive Social Security must have the Part B premiums automatically deducted from their Social Security checks. Part D participants may choose to have their premiums deducted from their Social Security checks.

Medicare premiums are absorbing a growing share of Social Security benefits. To see the effect of growing premiums, consider a Social Security beneficiary who earned the average wage throughout his or her career. If this retiree chose to participate in Part B—as the vast majority of Social Security beneficiaries do—the standard Part B premium would have absorbed almost 5% of benefits upon retirement in 2000 and about 8.5% in 2010 after over a decade of retirement. For a new retiree in 2010, the Part B premium absorbs about 9% of the Social Security benefit, and combined premiums for both Part B and Part D absorb about 12% of the average initial Social Security benefit check. Medicare's trustees project that premiums for Parts B and D will grow at a faster rate than average Social Security benefits in the future, thus consuming a greater proportion of benefits over time. In 2078, a retired worker receiving the average initial Social Security benefit amount is projected to need 22% of benefits to pay the Part B premium and 31% of initial benefits to pay combined Parts B and D premiums.

The deduction of Medicare premiums affects beneficiaries differently, depending on their Social Security benefit amounts and total incomes. Medicare premiums absorb a greater fraction of lower earners' Social Security benefits than of higher earners' benefits, because although benefit amounts are progressive, low earners tend to have lower dollar amounts of benefits. However, some low-income beneficiaries are eligible for subsidies that cover their Medicare premiums and other out-of-pocket costs. Other beneficiaries may be protected by a hold harmless provision that prevents a beneficiary's Social Security check from declining due to Part B premium increases.

The Social Security Administration (SSA) has announced that there will be no Social Security cost-of-living adjustment (COLA) in 2010, and both SSA and the Congressional Budget Office predict that there will be no COLA in 2011. Over the same period, total Medicare Part B program costs and premiums are expected to increase. In a typical year, the hold harmless provision affects a small fraction of beneficiaries. However, in a scenario where there is no Social Security COLA, the effects of the hold harmless provision are larger and more complex. For more information on this issue, please see CRS Report R40561, *The Effect of No Social Security COLA on Medicare Part B Premiums*, by Jim Hahn and Alison Shelton.

Finally, it is important to note that although Social Security beneficiaries are affected by rising health care costs, the benefits of participating in Medicare are substantially greater than the costs.

INTRODUCTION

Social Security and Medicare are large and important parts of America's safety net. About 45 million older and disabled individuals—1 in 7 Americans—are beneficiaries of both Social Security and Medicare.[1] Social Security and Medicare account for a large amount of federal spending. For 2010, spending on the two programs is projected at about $1.2 trillion, about 35% of outlays and about 8.4% of gross domestic product (GDP), one measure of the size of the U.S. economy.[2] Although Social Security and Medicare both play important roles in the well-being of older and disabled Americans, the interactions between the two programs are rarely examined.

This chapter focuses on how Medicare premiums affect Social Security beneficiaries. Medicare premiums are rising faster than Social Security benefits and are consequently consuming an increasing share of benefits over time.

Rising Medicare premiums could have a large effect on Social Security beneficiaries, particularly on those with low incomes and those who rely on Social Security as their primary source of income. Some beneficiaries may have more difficulty paying for rising health care costs than others. For example, among Americans aged 65 and older, 50% of married couples and 72% of unmarried persons receive more than half of their income from Social Security, and 20% of married couples and about 41% of unmarried persons receive more than 90% of their income from Social Security. [3] Some of these beneficiaries may see a decline in their standard of living as their Medicare premiums rise.

This chapter shows how the deduction of Medicare Part B and Part D premiums affects Social Security beneficiaries.[4] It describes how increases in Social Security benefits and Medicare premiums are calculated under current law and explains the circumstances under which many Social Security beneficiaries are held harmless for increases in the standard Part B premium, as well as the premium assistance available to low-income beneficiaries. It shows the growth in Social Security benefits and Part B premiums in recent years and describes how rising Part B premiums have affected Social Security beneficiaries with different levels of earnings, including both current beneficiaries and new enrollees. It also provides estimates of Social Security benefits and Medicare Parts B and D premiums to 2078, using the Social Security and Medicare trustees' intermediate projections, and describes how beneficiaries would be affected by projected Medicare premium increases.

BACKGROUND

Social Security Benefits

Social Security provides retirement, disability, and survivors benefits to workers and their families. People become insured for benefits by working in Social Security-covered employment (i.e., by paying Social Security payroll taxes).[5] Generally, people who qualify for retirement benefits may receive reduced Social Security benefits as early as age 62 or full benefits at the full retirement age.[6] Those who qualify for disability or certain survivors benefits may receive them at any age.[7] The amount of a worker's Social Security benefit is calculated by applying a progressive benefit formula to his or her lifetime earnings, adjusted for wage growth. Historically, the average Social Security benefit paid to new beneficiaries has increased at about the same rate as average earnings.

Annual Cost-of-Living Adjustment

After a person becomes eligible to receive Social Security benefits, his or her monthly benefit amount is increased annually to maintain purchasing power over time. Near the end of each year, the Social Security Administration (SSA) announces the cost-of-living adjustment (COLA) payable in January of the following year. The amount of the COLA is based on inflation as measured by the Consumer Price Index-Urban Wage Earners and Clerical Workers (CPI-W).[8] If the CPI-W decreases, Social Security benefits stay the same—benefits are not reduced during periods of deflation.

COLAs for 2010 and 2011

SSA has announced that there will be no Social Security COLA in 2010, and both SSA and the Congressional Budget Office predict that there will be no COLA in 2011.[9] For more on this subject and how this could affect Medicare Part B premiums, see CRS Report R40561, *The Effect of No Social Security COLA on Medicare Part B Premiums*, by Jim Hahn and Alison M. Shelton.

Medicare Premiums

Medicare is the federal health insurance program for people aged 65 and older and for certain disabled people. Medicare is composed of four parts:

- Part A: Hospital Insurance (HI);
- Part B: Supplementary Medical Insurance (SMI), which covers physician services and other outpatient expenses;
- Part C: Medicare Advantage (MA), which covers the same services as Parts A and B through private health insurance plans; and
- Part D: prescription drugs, which are covered through private plans.

Participation in Part A is required for Social Security beneficiaries aged 65 and older and for those who have received disability benefits for more than 24 months.[10] Part A beneficiaries may choose to participate in Parts B, C, and D.[11]

Medicare is funded through a combination of payroll taxes, general revenues, and beneficiary premiums. Medicare Part A is funded primarily through the payroll taxes of current workers and their employers, which are credited to the HI trust fund.[12] Parts B and D are financed through a combination of beneficiary premiums and federal general revenues, which are credited to the SMI trust fund. Part C is financed through the HI and SMI trust funds; Part C participants must pay the Part B premium.[13] Because this chapter focuses on the payment of Medicare premiums, the analysis herein primarily relates to Parts B and D.

Part B Premiums

At the end of each year, the Centers for Medicare and Medicaid Services (CMS) announce Part B premiums for the next year. The Balanced Budget Act of 1997 permanently set standard Part B premiums to cover 25% of projected per capita Part B program costs for beneficiaries aged 65 and older. [14] If projected Part B costs increase or decrease, the premium rises or falls proportionately. Unless they qualify for low-income assistance, Part B participants must pay monthly premiums; they must also pay other out-of-pocket costs when they use Part B services.

Starting in 2007, higher-income beneficiaries have paid higher Part B premiums.[15] Less than 5% of Part B beneficiaries will pay income-related premiums in 2010.[16]

Part B Premiums for 2010

In 2010, the standard Part B premium is $110.50 per month, up from $96.40 per month in 2009. In 2010, individuals whose modified adjusted gross income (AGI) exceeds $85,000, and couples whose modified AGI exceeds $170,000, are subject to higher premium amounts, as shown in **Table 1** below.[17] The analysis in this chapter focuses on the standard Part B premium of $110.50, which is paid by most beneficiaries. In addition to premiums, Part B beneficiaries must also pay other out-of-pocket costs when they use services. The annual deductible for Part B services is $155 in 2010. After the annual deductible is met, beneficiaries are responsible for coinsurance costs, which are generally 20% of Medicare-approved Part B expenses.

Table 1. Part B Premiums, 2010

Modified Adjusted Gross Income (AGI)		
Single	**Couple**	**Premium**
$85,000 or less	$170,000 or less	$110.50
$85,001-$107,000	$170,001-$214,000	$154.70
$107,001-$160,000	$214,001-$320,000	$221.00
$160,001-$213,000	$320,001-$426,000	$287.30
More than $213,000	More than 426,000	$353.60

Source: Social Security Administration, Medicare Part B Premiums: Important Information For People Newly Eligible For Medicare 2010, January 2010, at http://www.ssa.gov/pubs/10162.pdf

Note: For more information, see CRS Report R40082, *Medicare: Part B Premiums*, by Jim Hahn.

Medicare Advantage (Part C)

Beneficiaries who are entitled to Medicare Part A and enrolled in Part B may choose to enroll in a private health insurance plan through Part C, also known as Medicare Advantage (MA), which provides health care coverage in lieu of traditional Medicare. In 2009, about 23% of Medicare beneficiaries were enrolled in Part C, mostly in managed care plans.[18] Medicare Advantage plans are generally required to offer the same services as Medicare Parts A and B. MA managed care organizations must also offer at least one Medicare Advantage-prescription drug plan (MA-PD) that includes drug coverage at least equivalent to standard coverage in Part D plans. (Beneficiaries enrolled in MA managed care plans may not enroll in a stand-alone Part D plan.)[19]

Part C Premiums

Medicare Advantage participants' total premium amounts may be higher or lower than the Part B premium. Although the law requires that MA participants pay the Part B premium, some plans subsidize the premium for their enrollees. Other plans require that enrollees pay the full Part B premium plus an additional premium directly to the plan sponsor.[20]

Part D Premiums

Medicare Part D was established in the Medicare Prescription Drug, Improvement, and Modernization Act of 2003 (MMA, P.L. 108-173) and began covering beneficiaries' prescription drugs through private plans in January 2006.[21] To participate in Part D, qualified individuals must enroll in a participating prescription drug plan. Unless they qualify for low-income assistance, Part D participants must pay monthly premiums; they must also pay other out-of-pocket costs when they use Part D services.

MMA established guidelines for *standard* Part D coverage, including specific deductible and coinsurance amounts and a formula for calculating average premiums. Individual prescription drug plans are also allowed to offer *alternative* coverage that has at least actuarially equivalent benefits. In other words, alternative coverage plans must pay, on average, equal or greater benefits per person than standard coverage plans. Alternative coverage plans may charge higher or lower premiums, deductibles, and coinsurance than standard coverage plans.[22] This chapter focuses on beneficiaries' premiums for *standard* Part D coverage, which vary by plan. On average, a beneficiary's premium covers about one-fourth of the value of a standard coverage plan and the federal government pays for the remaining three-fourths.

Part D Premiums for 2009

The average premium for standard Part D coverage is $30 in 2010, up from $28 in 2009. The annual deductible for standard coverage is $310 in 2010. After meeting the deductible, beneficiaries pay 25% coinsurance costs for drug costs up to $2,830, all of their drug costs between $2,830 and $6,440, and about 5% of drug costs above $6,440.[23]

Medicare Premium Subsidies for Low-Income Beneficiaries

The analysis in this chapter focuses on Social Security beneficiaries who pay Medicare premiums. However, low-income individuals (including MA participants) may qualify for low-income subsidies, that cover all or part of their Part B and Part D premiums.[24] As of early 2009, about 8.8 million low-income Medicare beneficiaries received full Part B premium subsidies, and 9.6 million receive Part D subsidies.[25] Some beneficiaries who qualified for premium subsidies did not apply for them.

To qualify for subsidies, beneficiaries must have limited income and assets. Beneficiaries may qualify for full Part B premium subsidies if they have incomes of less than 135% of poverty and assets of less than $4,000 for an individual or $6,000 for a couple. Beneficiaries may qualify for full or partial Part D premium subsidies if they have incomes of less than 150% of poverty and assets of less than $12,510 for an individual and $25,010 for a couple in 2010.[26]

Hold Harmless Provision for Medicare Part B Premiums

A *hold harmless* provision reduces the Part B premium for most beneficiaries whose Social Security COLAs are not sufficient to cover the standard Part B premium increase.[27] If, in a given year, the increase in the standard Part B premium would cause a beneficiary's Social Security check to be less, in dollar terms, than it was the year before, then the Part B premium is reduced to ensure that the nominal amount of the individual's Social Security check stays the same.[28]

Several groups are *not* covered by the hold harmless provision. New enrollees to either Medicare or Social Security, as well as Part B enrollees who do not receive Social Security benefits, will pay higher Part B premiums without protection from the hold harmless provision.[29] High-income individuals, who pay income-related Part B premiums instead of the standard premium, are not protected by the hold harmless provision and may see reduced Social Security checks from one year to the next as a result of an increase in the Part B premium. Low-income beneficiaries are not held harmless, but because they also do not pay the Part B premium—Medicaid pays the premiums for them—the costs of low-income beneficiaries' rising Part B premiums will generally be borne by state governments instead of by the beneficiaries themselves.[30]

Whether a beneficiary is held harmless depends on the amount of the standard Part B premium increase relative to the amount of his or her Social Security COLA in a given year; this determination is made by SSA. As described earlier, an individual's Social Security COLA is determined by multiplying his or her benefit amount by the inflation rate (i.e., the CPI-W). Part B premiums are determined by projected Part B program costs. Thus, the number of people held harmless can vary widely from year to year, depending on annual inflation rates and projected Part B costs.[31]

In some cases, a beneficiary may be held harmless one year but not the next. In other cases, a beneficiary will be held harmless in a current year because his or her Part B premium was reduced in an earlier year. The cumulative effect of the hold harmless provision can produce substantial savings for individuals with low benefits.

A beneficiary is *not* held harmless if the increase in his or her Part D premium (or the combined increase in Part B and Part D premiums) causes his or her Social Security check to decline. In other words, a person's Social Security check may decrease from one year to the next as a result of Part D premium increases.

No Social Security COLA Scenario

SSA announced on October 15, 2009, that there will be no Social Security COLA in 2010. Furthermore, both SSA and the Congressional Budget Office predict that there will be no COLA in 2011. Over the same period, total Medicare Part B program costs and premiums are expected to increase.[32] In a typical year, the hold harmless provision affects a small fraction of beneficiaries and has a limited impact on program finances. However, in a scenario where Medicare Part B premiums increase but Social Security benefits do not, the effects of the hold harmless provision are larger and more complex. For more information on this issue, please see CRS Report R40561, *The Effect of No Social Security COLA on Medicare Part B Premiums*, by Jim Hahn and Alison M. Shelton.

Growth in Social Security Benefits and Medicare Part B Premiums from 2001 to 2010

Figure 1 shows the annual rates of increase in Medicare premiums and Social Security retiree benefits (reflecting COLA increases) from 2001 to 2010. The cumulative growth in standard Part B premiums has been dramatic, but annual changes have been somewhat erratic. During the past 10 years, annual Part B premium increases have ranged from 0% to more than 17%. Social Security COLAs, meanwhile, have ranged from 0% to 5.8%. In 2009, there was no Part B premium increase and in 2010, there was no COLA

For a worker who retired in 2001, the percentage increase in the Part B premium exceeded the Social Security COLA in each year through 2008. In dollar terms, which increase is greater would vary from individual to individual, depending on how the dollar amount of the Part B premium increase compares to the dollar amount of a given individual's COLA (which in turn depends on the dollar amount of his or her benefit before the COLA increase).

Historical Benefit Thresholds for the Hold Harmless Provision

As discussed above, a *hold harmless* provision reduces the Part B premium for most beneficiaries whose Social Security COLAs are not sufficient to cover the standard Part B premium increase.

Figure 2 shows approximate Social Security hold harmless threshold amounts from 2001 to 2009. The majority of Social Security participants with monthly benefit amounts below the thresholds were held harmless, whereas participants with monthly benefit amounts above this threshold were not held harmless. In particular, for monthly Social Security benefit amounts below these thresholds, the dollar amount of the Part B premium increase was greater than the dollar amount of the Social Security benefit increase (which in turn is the previous year's Social Security benefit times the COLA), so that the net Social Security benefit would have fallen relative to the previous year's benefit in the absence of the hold harmless provision. To prevent a decline in the Social Security benefit from one year to the next, the Part B premium increase is reduced for most beneficiaries with monthly Social Security benefits below the threshold.[33] If a beneficiary had benefits above the threshold in a given year, he or she would pay the full Part B premium increase in that year. In 2010, there is no Social Security COLA, therefore the hold harmless provision applies to all beneficiaries except for the previously noted groups.

IMPACT OF MEDICARE PREMIUMS ON SOCIAL SECURITY BENEFICIARIES

Ultimately, almost everyone who is eligible for Social Security retirement or disability benefits qualifies for Medicare.[34] Most people who elect to participate in the Part B or Part D programs pay premiums.[35] By law, the Medicare Part B premium is automatically deducted from the Social Security benefits of those enrolled in Part B (including MA and MA-PD participants).[36] Medicare Part D participants may choose to have their Part D premiums deducted from their benefits or to pay them directly to their prescription drug plan sponsors.

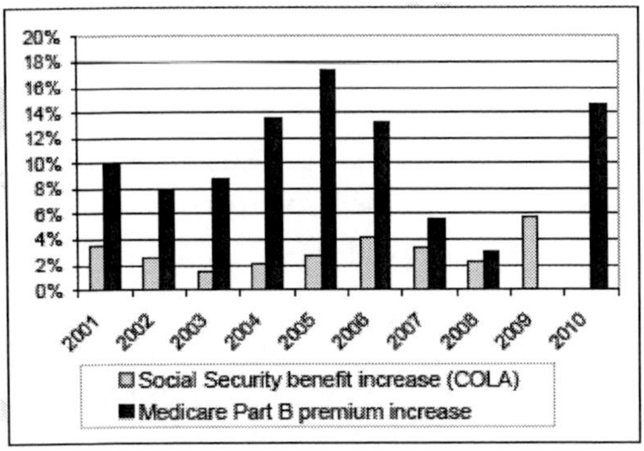

Source: 2009 Medicare Trustees Report and the *2009 Social Security Trustees Report, updated for 2010 Part B premium and announcement of no 2010 Social Security COLA.*

Note: There were no increases in the Part B premium in 2009 and the Social Security COLA was zero in 2010.

Figure 1. Annual Percent Increase in Social Security Benefits and Standard Medicare Part B Premiums, 2001-2010

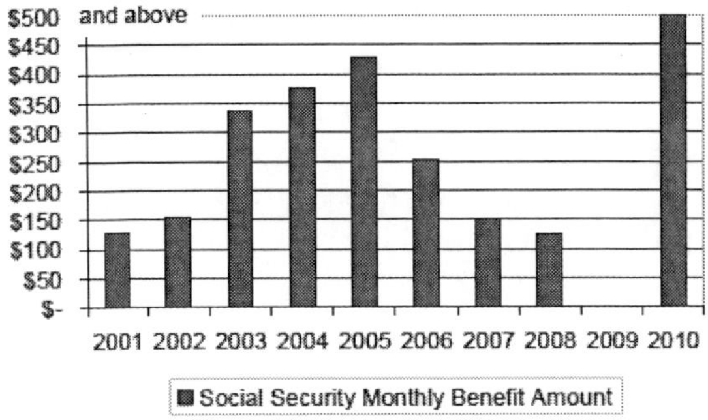

Source: Congressional Research Service calculations, based on figures from *the 2009 Medicare Trustees Report and the 2009 Social Security Trustees Report, updated for reported 2010 Part B premium and announcement of no 2010 Social Security COLA*.

Notes: There was no increases in the Medicare Part B premium in 2009 so the hold harmless provision did not apply. In 2010, there was no Social Security COLA so the hold harmless provision applied to all Social Security benefit amounts except for excluded categories of beneficiaries, as described above.

Figure 2. Approximate Social Security Benefit Thresholds for Hold Harmless Provision, 2001-2010

For new enrollees, the full amount of the Part B premium, including any annual increase, is subtracted from the Social Security benefit. New enrollees are not held harmless from Part B premiums increases, as described above. Initial Social Security benefits generally increase in line with national wage growth; in other words, as successive cohorts of workers retire each year, each cohort's initial benefits is somewhat higher as a reflection of the wage growth it experienced while working. Over the past decade, initial benefits have increased by about 37%. During the same period, standard Part B premiums have more than doubled, from $50.00 in 2001 to $110.50 in 2010, an increase of 12 1%.

Once a person has retired, his or her Social Security benefit is indexed to inflation and thereafter grows with annual Social Security COLAs. A "hold harmless" provision, described below, caps the Part B premium increase (but not the Part D increase) at the dollar amount of a beneficiary's COLA. Over the past decade, Social Security's annual COLA resulted in a cumulative benefit increase of about 31%, less than the Part B premium growth of 121%.[37]

Impact on the Cohort that Retired in 2000

The following section illustrates how the deduction of Medicare Part B premiums would have affected the Social Security benefits of three hypothetical workers who retired in 2000 and received Social Security benefits, increased for the annual COLA, through 2010.[38] The three workers are a low earner, a medium earner, and a high earner.[39] The *low earner* is assumed to have earned 45% of the average wage during each year of his or her career (about $19,553 in 20 10) and to receive a monthly Social Security benefit of about $800 in 2010.[40] The *medium earner* is assumed to have earned the average wage during each year of his or her career (about $43,451 in 2010) and to receive a monthly Social Security benefit of about $1,300 in 2010. The high earner is assumed to have earned 160% of the average wage during each year of his or her career (about $69,522 in 2010) and to receive a monthly Social Security benefit of $1,700 in 2010. All of the hypothetical workers are assumed to have been born in 1935, to have worked full-time each year from the ages of 22 to 65 with no interruptions, to have retired in 2000 at the age of 65, and to pay the standard Part B premium without low-income assistance or protection under the hold harmless provision.[41]

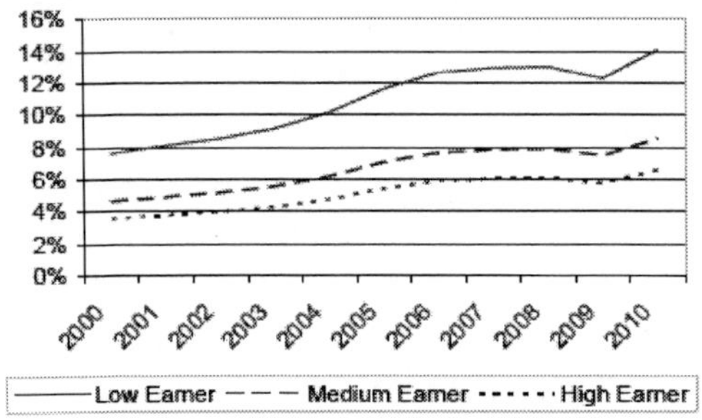

Source: Congressional Research Service calculations, based on figures from the *2009 Medicare Trustees Report and the 2009 Social Security Trustees Report, updated for reported 2010 Part B premium and announcement of no 2010 Social Security COLA..*

Note: The calculations in this figure are based on individuals who retired in 2000. Estimates for other cohorts would vary.

Figure 3. Percentage of Total Social Security Benefits Deducted for Standard Part B Premiums, 2000-2010

Figure 3 shows the percentage of each hypothetical retired worker's Social Security benefits that was deducted to pay the standard Part B premium, for a single cohort of workers who retired in 2000 and continued to receive Social Security benefits, increased for the COLA, through 2010.

As shown in Figure 3, a growing proportion of Social Security benefits have been deducted to pay Part B premiums over the 11-year period. In 2000, the medium earner needed approximately 4.6% of his or her Social Security benefits to pay the Part B premium each year. By 2010, after 11 years of retirement, the Part B premium absorbed about 8.5% of the medium earner's benefits. In other words, the proportion of benefits needed to pay the standard Part B premium nearly doubled over the past decade.

Lower earners need a greater fraction of their Social Security benefits to pay the Part B premium than do higher earners. For example, in 2010 the low earner in this illustration needs about 14% of his or her Social Security benefit check to pay the Part B premium. In contrast, the high earner needs about 7% of his or her benefit check to pay the Part B premium. Although Social Security benefits are progressive, they are also based on a workers' lifetime earnings; consequently, low earners are disproportionately affected by the deduction of Medicare premiums. Some low earners may be protected by Medicaid's Part B premium subsidies for low-income beneficiaries.

Note that the share of the Social Security benefit absorbed by the Part B premium from 2000 to 2010 in Figure 3 increased despite the hold harmless provision. Effectively, the Part B premium increase absorbed part of the COLA each year, as described in Figure 4 below, but the dollar amount of the premium increase did not exceed the dollar amount of COLA in any of the years (except 2010), so the hold harmless provision was not triggered for any of the example workers until 2010 (when it was triggered for most workers).[42]

Figure 4 shows, for the same hypothetical workers shown in Figure 3, how much of the Social Security COLA was absorbed by the Part B premium increase in each year. The premium clearly absorbed more of the COLA in some years than in others. For example, in 2005 the Part B premium increase absorbed about 40% of the medium earner's COLA. In 2000 and 2009, there was no Part B premium increase, so beneficiaries kept their entire Social Security COLAs. In years with premium increases, those with lower benefits need a greater fraction of their Social Security COLAs to cover the Part B premium increase than those with higher benefits. In 2010 (not shown in Figure 4), the absence of a Social Security COLA means that for the typical worker the Medicare Part B premium will not be allowed to increase.

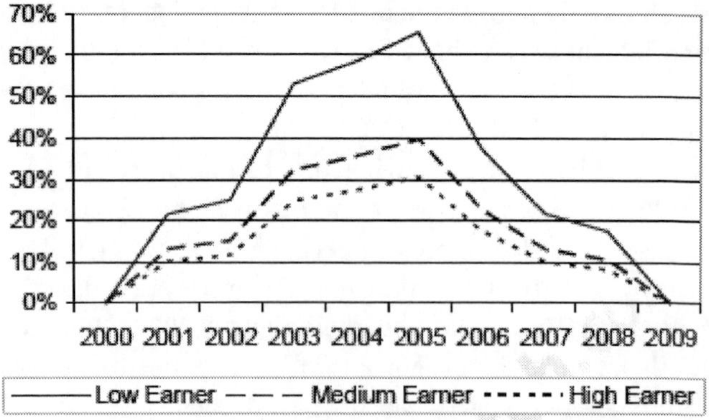

Source: Congressional Research Service calculations, based on figures from the *2009 Medicare Trustees Report and the 2009 Social Security Trustees Report, updated for reported 2010 Part B premium and announcement of no 2010 Social Security COLA.*

Notes: The calculations in this figure are based on individuals who retired in 2000. Estimates for other cohorts would vary. There were no increases in the Medicare Part B premium in 2000 or 2009, and no Social Security COLA in 2010 (not shown because the ratio of Part B premiums to the COLA for 2010 would involve dividing by zero).

Figure 4. Percentage of Social Security COLAs Absorbed by Standard Part B Increase, 2000-2009

Impact on Initial Benefits of Cohorts Retiring in Each Year from 2010 to 2078

Looking forward, most experts agree that Medicare cost growth will continue to outstrip growth in prices (and thus Social Security COLAs for existing beneficiaries) and wages (and thus initial Social Security benefits for new beneficiaries). The trustees of Social Security and Medicare project that over the long term, annual inflation will average 2.8%, annual wage growth will average 3.9%, and annual increases in Parts B and D costs per beneficiary will average 5% or more. Long-range projections are inherently imprecise; the further into the future one looks, the wider the range of possible outcomes. Projections of Medicare cost growth are particularly uncertain. Sources of uncertainty range from the difficulty of predicting medical breakthroughs to the ongoing implementation of Part D. In fact, many experts believe that Part B costs will grow faster than the trustees have projected.

Why the Trustees' Projections of Medicare Part B Premiums May Be Too Low

Trustees Assume Cuts to Physician Payments. The Medicare trustees make their projections of future program costs and premiums based on the provisions of the law that authorizes Medicare. The law requires a sustainable growth rate (SGR) formula to be used to calculate Medicare physician payments, which account for about 50% of Part B costs. Application of this formula would result in cuts to physician fees of about 21% in 2010 and by additional amounts in subsequent years. The Medicare trustees assume that these cuts will be made.

However, congressional action has prevented cuts to physician fees for 2003 to 2009. Many Members of Congress were concerned about the impact of potential payment reductions on beneficiaries' access to services. The trustees acknowledge that "multiple years of significant reductions in physician payments per service are very unlikely to occur before legislative changes intervene." If the trustees had not assumed that physician payments would be cut, projected Part B costs would be significantly higher. Consequently, projected Part B premiums would be higher, because they are proportionate to projected program costs.

Trustees Assume Medicare Cost Growth Will Slow. The Medicare trustees assume that the growth in Medicare costs (and thus premiums) will slow in the future. The Congressional Budget Office (CBO) explains that "in their long range forecasts, the Medicare trustees assume that the development and increasing use of new medical technologies will cause spending per enrollee to continue to grow faster than [inflation and wages] but that significant pressures will be brought to bear on the entire health-care system to reduce [costs]." Consequently, the trustees project that the growth in Medicare premiums will also slow. The trustees' intermediate projection is that Part B premiums will increase by an average annual rate of at least 5% over the long term.

Many experts believe this projected growth rate is too low. One reason is that the trustees' projections are significantly lower than past growth rates for Part B premiums. If Part B premiums continue to rise at the same rate as they have in the past, they will increase much more rapidly than the Medicare trustees project.

Sources: 2009 Medicare Trustees Report; CBO, The Long-Term Budget Outlook, December 2007; and CBO, *The Budget and Economic Outlook: Fiscal Years 2010 to 2020.*

Uncertainties in Projecting Part D Premiums

How will drug prices and utilization change? Changes in drug prices and utilization could have a significant impact on Part D premiums. If generic drugs become increasingly available or more widely used, premiums could be lower than expected. Alternatively, pharmaceutical breakthroughs or increased use of expensive prescriptions could lead to higher premiums.

How many prescription drug plans will compete for beneficiaries? In the first several years of implementation, a greater-than-expected number of plans offered Part D benefits. If a large number of plans continue to offer Part D benefits, competition to attract beneficiaries could drive down premiums. Alternatively, some analysts believe that the fierce competition for beneficiaries will force some plans out of Part D in future years, reducing competition and leading to higher premiums.

It is also difficult to project how Medicare Part D premiums, implemented in 2006, might change over time. (See the text box.) Early estimates of Part D costs varied widely. The nature of Part D makes it difficult to project premiums, because individual plans set premiums for their beneficiaries. In general, prescription drug spending has been rising at least as much as overall health spending; this trend is expected to continue.

Figure 5 shows the proportion of the average Social Security benefit that would be needed to pay standard Part B premiums from 2010 to 2078, for new enrollees to Social Security and Medicare in each of these years. It also shows the proportion of the average Social Security benefit that would be needed to pay the combined standard Part B and average premium for standard Part D coverage. The graph is based on the trustees' intermediate projections. Each year in the graph shows the projected percentage of average Social Security benefits that would be needed to pay Medicare premiums *for a person who turned 65 and retired in January of that year*. In interpreting Figure 5, it is important to note that Part D premiums vary widely by plan, and that Part D premiums may be deducted from beneficiaries' Social Security checks or be paid directly to the plan.

The estimates in Figure 5 show the proportion of *initial* Social Security benefits needed to pay Medicare premiums for a series of different cohorts retiring in each year from 2010 to 2078. As noted above, the initial Social Security benefits received by new enrollees generally rise in line with wage growth, so that cohorts retiring in successive years will each receive somewhat higher initial benefits than the previous cohorts. After the initial year of benefits, a retiree's Social Security benefits are indexed to inflation using the COLA, so that for a single cohort retiring in a given year, all future benefits rise with inflation. Thus, Figure 5 below represents the initial benefits of different cohorts retiring in successive years, whereas Figure 3 represented a single cohort for whom the Part B premium was deducted each year from the COLA-indexed benefit. On average, Medicare premiums have grown faster than both wages and prices and are projected to do so in the future.

Beneficiaries are projected to need a much larger fraction of their Social Security benefits to pay Part B premiums in the future. For example, in 2011 it is projected that the Part B premium will absorb 11% of the average initial Social Security benefit in the first year of retirement, and the combined Parts B and D premiums will absorb 14% of the average initial benefit. In 2078 premiums are projected to absorb more than twice that share, with 22% going to pay the Part B premium in the first year of retirement, and 31% of the average initial benefit in the first year of retirement going to pay combined

Parts B and D premiums. In the future, as in the past, low earners will need a greater fraction of their benefits to pay the Part B premium than will high earners.

LEGISLATION IN THE 111TH CONGRESS

As a result of SSA's announcement that no COLA will be paid in 2010, and if, as projected, there is no Social Security COLA in 2011, then a range of issues may potentially be addressed through legislation. These issues may include the impact of the hold harmless provision on the Part B premiums paid by beneficiaries who are not held harmless, the impact on seniors who will pay higher Part D premiums and higher out-of-pocket medical costs, and other issues. Several bills before the 111th Congress would address one or more of these issues. For more information, please see CRS Report R40561, *The Effect of No Social Security COLA on Medicare Part B Premiums*, by Jim Hahn and Alison M. Shelton.

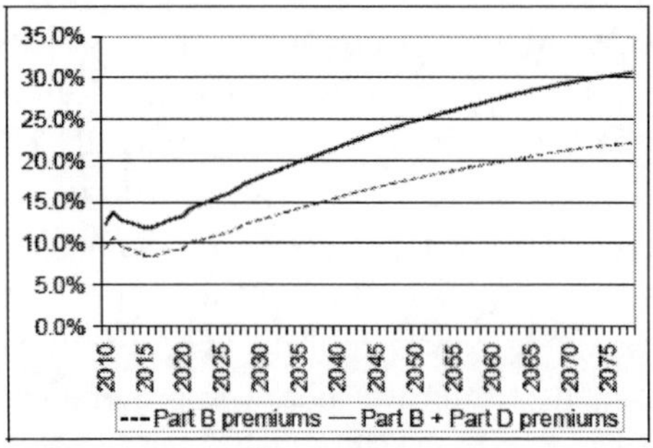

Source: 2009 Medicare Trustees Report, Figure III.C 1.

Note: Part B premiums are not expected to decrease as a proportion of Social Security benefits, as they are shown to do in the early years of Figure 5. Figure 5 is based on the trustees' projections; the trustees acknowledge that their short-run projections of Part B costs are "unrealistically reduced" due to the assumption that physician payments will be cut (2009 Medicare Trustees Report, p. 31). Figure 5 shows different cohorts of hypothetical workers each year in the first year of their retirements.

Figure 5. Percentage of Average Initial Social Security Benefits Deducted for Standard Medicare Part B and Part D Premiums, 2010-2078

CONCLUSION

Rising Medicare premiums are consuming a growing share of beneficiaries' Social Security benefits. An increasing number of Americans will be affected by this interaction as the number of Social Security and Medicare beneficiaries grows over time. The Social Security trustees project that by 2040, the proportion of Americans aged 65 and older—most of whom are eligible for both Social Security and Medicare—will almost double.[43]

Low-income beneficiaries and those who rely primarily on Social Security may see a decline in their standard of living as their Medicare expenses rise. Premiums for Parts B and D are projected to increase significantly faster than Social Security benefits. As a result, the Part B and Part D premiums are projected to consume a growing share of the annual Social Security COLA, which was designed to maintain beneficiaries' living standards.

Some beneficiaries will be protected from rising Medicare premiums: Medicaid covers premiums for some persons who meet income and asset tests, and the hold harmless provision protects most Social Security beneficiaries against Part B increases (although not Part D increases) that exceed the annual Social Security COLA. Many beneficiaries could struggle to cover their health care expenses, however, including new enrollees who are not covered by the hold harmless provision.[44]

Out-of-pocket costs for Parts B and D are projected to grow at the same rates as premiums, contributing to the growing health care expenses of beneficiaries. Most beneficiaries are likely to have some income apart from their Social Security benefits. However, many of tomorrow's beneficiaries, like today's, are likely to rely mostly on Social Security, especially as traditional pension coverage declines and many Americans save little or nothing for retirement.[45]

Finally, it is important to remember that Social Security beneficiaries gain from their participation in the Medicare program. Medicare provides health care coverage to the vast majority of Americans aged 65 and older and to most disability beneficiaries. Together, Medicare and Medicaid cover a majority of participating Social Security beneficiaries' health care expenses. Although Social Security beneficiaries are affected by rising health care costs, the benefits of participating in Medicare are substantially greater than the costs.

End Notes

[1] Social Security Administration, 2009 Annual Report of the Board of Trustees of the Federal Old-Age and Survivors Insurance and Disability Insurance Trust Funds, May 12, 2009, at http://www.ssa.gov/OACT/TR/2009/tr09.pdf. (Hereafter cited as 2009 Social Security Trustees Report.) Centers for Medicare and Medicaid Services, 2009 Annual Report of the Boards of Trustees of the Federal Hospital Insurance and Federal Supplementary Medical Insurance Trust Funds, May 12, 2009, available at http://www.cms.hhs.gov/ReportsTrustFunds/downloads/tr2009.pdf. (Hereafter cited as 2009 Medicare Trustees Report.)

[2] Congressional Budget Office, *The Budget and Economic Outlook: Fiscal Years 2010 to 2020*, January 2010, Table 3- 1, at http://www.cbo.gov/ftpdocs/108xx/doc10871/01-26-Outlook.pdf.

[3] http://www.ssa.gov/pressoffice/basicfact.htm

[4] Medicare Part B, Supplementary Medical Insurance (SMI), covers physician services and other outpatient expenses. Medicare Part D covers prescription drugs through private plans.

[5] The amount of time a person must work in Social Security-covered employment to be insured for benefits depends on the type of benefit, among other factors. For more details, see CRS Report 94-27, *Social Security: Brief Facts and Statistics*, by Gary Sidor.

[6] The age at which workers may receive full retirement benefits is rising from 65 (for those born before 1938) to 67 (for those born after 1959).

[7] Social Security also provides benefits to a worker's family, such as spouse benefits and survivor benefits, that are based on the lifetime earnings of the worker. For more information, see CRS Report 94-27, *Social Security: Brief Facts and Statistics*, by Gary Sidor.

[8] The CPI-W tracks the prices of a fixed market basket of goods and services over time. Social Security's COLA is calculated as the change in the CPI-W from the third quarter of the prior calendar year to the third quarter of the current calendar year. If the CPI-W increases during this period, Social Security benefits for the next year increase proportionately. See CRS Report 94-803, *Social Security: Cost-of-Living Adjustments*, by Gary Sidor and CRS Report RL30074, *The Consumer Price Index: A Brief Overview*, by Brian W. Cashell.

[9] http://www.socialsecurity.gov/pressoffice/factsheets/colafacts2010.htm.

[10] People who receive Social Security benefits that confer eligibility for Part A (i.e., retirement benefits for those aged 65 and older and disability benefits after 24 months) may not waive Part A entitlement. (Social Security Administration, Program Operations Manual System, HI 0080 1.002, at https://s044a90.ssa.gov/apps10/poms.nsf/lnx/ 0600801002! opendocument.)

[11] Of Part A beneficiaries, roughly 94% are enrolled in Part B, and about 22% are enrolled in Part C. In 2008, about 90% of Medicare beneficiaries had prescription drug coverage of some kind. About 25 million were enrolled in standalone Part D plans or had prescription drug coverage through their Part C plans, and an additional 14 million were enrolled in other health insurance plans that were subsidized by Part D. (CRS Report RL34280, *Medicare Part D Prescription Drug Benefit: A Primer*, by Jennifer O'Sullivan.)

[12] About 99% of Medicare beneficiaries qualify for premium-free Part A coverage, which they earn if they (or their spouses) have worked at least 10 years in Medicare-covered employment. Individuals without sufficient work history who are otherwise eligible for Medicare may participate in the program if they pay monthly Part A premiums.

[13] The law requires that Part C participants pay the Part B premium. Some Part C plans subsidize the premium for their enrollees; others require that enrollees pay the full Part B premium plus an additional premium directly to the plan sponsor.

[14] Disabled Medicare beneficiaries under age 65 pay the same premium amount as those aged 65 or older, though their per capita Part B costs are higher.

[15] The Medicare Prescription Drug, Improvement, and Modernization Act of 2003 (P.L. 108-173) increased the Part B premium percentage for high-income enrollees; the Deficit Reduction Act of 2005 (P.L. 109-17 1) accelerated the phase-in period for such premiums.

[16] SSA, Medicare Part B Premiums: Important Information For People Newly Eligible For Medicare 2010, January 2010, at http://www.ssa.gov/pubs/10162.pdf.

[17] For more information, see CRS Report R40082, *Medicare: Part B Premiums*, by Jim Hahn.

[18] Kaiser Family Foundation, *Fact Sheet: Medicare Advantage*, November 2009, at http://www.kff.org/medicare/ upload/2052-13.pdf.

[19] MA providers of nonmanaged care plans (i.e., private fee-for-service [PFFS] plans and medical savings accounts [MSAs]) are *not* required to offer prescription drug coverage. Drug coverage is optional for PFFS providers; PFFS plan enrollees without drug coverage are permitted to enroll in a stand-alone Part D plan. MSAs may not offer drug coverage.

[20] As of early 2009, about half (49%) of MA participants' total premiums were equal to the Part B premium amount, and about half (49%) paid higher premiums. About 2% paid lower premiums. (AARP Public Policy Institute, *A First Look at How Medicare Advantage Benefits and Premiums in Individual Enrollment Plans Are Changing from 2008 to 2009,* by Marsha Gold and Maria Cupples Hudson, March 2009, at http://assets.aarp.org /rgcenter/health/ i25_medicare.pdf.)

[21] See CRS Report RL3 1966, *Overview of the Medicare Prescription Drug, Improvement, and Modernization Act of 2003*, by Jennifer O'Sullivan et al. and CRS Report RL3 1525, *Beneficiary Cost-Sharing Under the Medicare Prescription Drug Benefit*, by Jim Hahn.

[22] For example, in 2010 premiums for all stand-alone Part D plans ranged from $8.80 to $120.20 per month (Kaiser Family Foundation, *Fact Sheet: The Medicare Prescription Drug Benefit*, November 2009, http://www.kff.org/ medicare/upload/7044-10.pdf hereafter cited as Kaiser, *Part D Fact Sheet*).

[23] The majority of plans offered to beneficiaries in 2009 were alternative coverage plans. Many of these plans include tiered cost-sharing, under which costs are lower for generic drugs and higher for brand-name drugs (Kaiser, *Part D Fact Sheet* and CMS, *Announcement of Calendar Year (CY) 2010 Medicare Advantage Capitation Rates and Medicare Advantage and Part D Payment Policies,* April 6, 2009, Attachment IV, available at http://www.cms.hhs.gov/MedicareAdvtgSpecRateStats/Downloads/Announcement2010. pdf).

[24] For more information on subsidies for low-income Medicare beneficiaries, see CRS Report R40082, *Medicare: Part B Premiums*, by Jim Hahn and CRS Report RL32902, *Medicare Prescription Drug Benefit: Low-Income Provisions*, by Jennifer O'Sullivan.

[25] Kaiser Family Foundation, *Dual Eligibles: Medicaid's Role for Low-Income Medicare Beneficiaries*, February 2009, at http://www.kff.org/medicaid/4091.cfm; Kaiser, *Part D Fact Sheet.*

[26] Centers for Medicare and Medicaid Services, *Medicare and You, 2010*, available at http://www.medicare.gov/ Publications/Pubs/pdf/10050.pdf#78.

[27] 42 U.S.C. § 1839(f). The hold harmless provision was first implemented in January 1987.

[28] If a beneficiary's benefit amount changes during a year in which he or she is held harmless (e.g., a beneficiary begins to be affected by the government pension offset), the Part B premium amount does *not* change. For more information on the hold harmless provision, see CRS Report R40561, *The Effect of No Social Security COLA on Medicare Part B Premiums*, by Jim Hahn and Alison Shelton.

[29] To be held harmless in a given year, a beneficiary must have had Part B premiums deducted from both the December check of the prior year and the January check of the current year.

[30] For more information on the hold harmless provision and the impact on Part B premiums if there is no Social Security COLA during 2010 and 2011, see CRS Report R40561, *The Effect of No Social Security COLA on Medicare Part B Premiums*, by Jim Hahn and Alison Shelton.

[31] For example, about 1.8 million Part B participants (6% of those paying premiums) were held harmless in 2005, and roughly 1 million participants (3% of those paying premiums) in 2006 (SSA Actuarial Note No. 147).

[32] By law, Medicare Part B premiums cover 25% of annual program costs.

[33] Some beneficiaries with benefits below these thresholds would *not* have had their Part B premiums reduced because their benefit checks would not have declined as a result of the Part B premium increase, due to the fact the Social Security benefits are rounded down to the nearest dollar. These thresholds apply only to beneficiaries who were not held harmless in the previous year. For more information, see SSA Actuarial Note No. 147.

[34] Generally, people aged 65 and older who qualify for Social Security benefits and people of any age who receive disability benefits (after a two-year waiting period) are entitled to Part A, with some exceptions. Part A beneficiaries are also eligible to enroll in Part B, in a private health insurance plan through Part C, and/or in a private prescription drug plan through Part D.

[35] Some beneficiaries do not pay Medicare premiums, either because they receive low-income assistance or because they choose not to enroll in Medicare Part B or Part D.

[36] 42 U.S.C. § 1840(a)(1). Part B premiums are also deducted from Railroad Retirement benefits (42 U.S.C. § 1 840(b)(1)).

[37] The COLA increases the benefits paid to *current* beneficiaries. In contrast, average Social Security benefits (those paid to new and current beneficiaries) have risen at a faster rate than the annual COLA, because the formula for calculating initial Social Security benefits is linked to *wage* growth, whereas the COLA is based on *price* growth. Generally, wages rise faster than prices.

[38] Part D premiums are not included in this example because Medicare Part D did not exist in 2000.

[39] The hypothetical workers were developed by SSA's actuaries. See Social Security Administration, Office of the Chief Actuary, Actuarial Note Number 144, *Internal Rates of Return Under the OASDI Program for Hypothetical Workers*, by Orlo R. Nichols et al., June 2001, at http://www.ssa.gov/OACT/NOTES/note2000s/note144.html.

[40] The *average wage* is defined by SSA's Average Wage Index (AWI), found in Table VI.F6 in the 2009 Trustees Report. The AWI tends to overestimate workers' lifetime earnings. See University of Michigan Retirement Research Center, Working Paper WP 2004-074, *Modeling Lifetime Earnings Paths: Hypothetical versus Actual Workers*, by Andrew Au, Olivia Mitchell, and John W.R. Phillips, March 2004, at *http://www.mrrc.isr.umich.edu /publications/* Papers/pdf/wp074.pdf.

[41] The low earner could potentially qualify for assistance in paying Part B premiums if he or she had little or no income besides Social Security benefits, had assets below the statutory limit ($4,000 for an individual and $6,000 for a couple), and applied for assistance.

[42] Consistent with this, the benefit levels of the three model workers, as described at the beginning of this section, are all higher than the hold harmless thresholds described in the figures.

[43] *2009 Social Security Trustees Report*, Table V.A2.

[44] For more information on the hold harmless provision and the impact on Part B premiums if there is no Social Security COLA for 2010 and 2011, see CRS Report R40561, *The Effect of No Social Security COLA on Medicare Part B Premiums*, by Jim Hahn and Alison Shelton.

[45] CRS Report RL30122, *Pension Sponsorship and Participation: Summary of Recent Trends* and CRS Report RL30922, *Retirement Savings and Household Wealth in 2007*, both by Patrick Purcell.

CHAPTER SOURCES

The following chapters have been previously published:

Chapter 1 – This is an edited, excerpted and augmented edition of a United States Congressional Research Service publication, Report Order Code RL33028, dated June 16, 2009.

Chapter 2 – This is an edited, excerpted and augmented edition of a United States Congressional Research Service publication, Report Order Code RS20607, dated January 12, 2010.

Chapter 3 – This is an edited, excerpted and augmented edition of a United States Congressional Research Service publication, Report Order Code RL30708, dated December 29, 2009.

Chapter 4 – This is an edited, excerpted and augmented edition of a United States Congressional Research Service publication, Report Order Code R41242, dated May 17, 2010.

Chapter 5 – This is an edited, excerpted and augmented edition of a United States Congressional Research Service publication, Report Order Code RL32896, dated February 17, 2010.

Chapter 6 – This is an edited, excerpted and augmented edition of a United States Congressional Research Service publication, Report Order Code RL33943, dated April 9, 2010.

Chapter 7 – This is an edited, excerpted and augmented edition of a United States Congressional Research Service publication, Report Order Code RL32552, dated January 15, 2010.

Chapter 8 – This is an edited, excerpted and augmented edition of a United States Congressional Research Service publication, Report Order Code RL33364, dated January 27, 2010.

INDEX

S

T

U

V

W